First Edition 2020

ISBN 978 1 9997175 8 2

British Library Cataloguing-in-Publication Data
A catalogue record for this book is available from the British Library.

Published by Destinworld Publishing Ltd.
www.destinworld.com

Cover design by John Wright
Maps by Simonetta Giori | simonettagiori@mac.com

This guide book is dedicated to:

Yorkshire Architectural and York Archaeological Society (YAYAS)

York Civic Trust

York Conservation Trust

and all those who work for the preservation

of York's unique

history, culture and heritage.

City of Churches! beautiful art Thou!
With all Thy steeples pointing to the Sky!
When from some neighb'ring hill's ascending brow,
We gaze upon Thee with affection's eye,
'Tis sweet to see Thee in the sunbeams lie,
Stretched out in calmness placid and serene,
Whilst some tall vessel, gliding slowly by,
Shows where Thy sparkling waters intervene,
And gives a lively change refreshing to the scene!
                              Lyra Eboracensis, 1839

Contents

Foreword

I n 2009 I moved to York when I married my husband, who introduced me to the delights of York. As the years have progressed I have become more and more interested in and enchanted by the multitudinous layers of history that this unique city has to offer. The twelve walks in this book are an attempt to share with you, in a direct and physical way, some of the amazing history of this two thousand year-old city. There's no substitute for learning about a place than actually being in it yourself.

Each walk is designed to take a morning or an afternoon, but could be extended with optional visits to many of the museums and places of interest that are mentioned. Opening times and prices vary, so websites have been included for you to check before you go.

Walk directions are designed to stand out in bold, while historical information is presented in normal text. As a keen walker in both cities and the countryside, it is a good tip to read a walk all the way through before you embark upon it, so that you have some idea of your route before having to deal with crowds of people, who may obscure your way. With approximately 6.9 million visitors to York per year, it is best to avoid doing the walks at busy periods, such as Saturdays and at Christmas time.

The walks are listed in loose chronological order. Each one is self-contained, so you could just dip in and out of whichever period interests you. Or you could complete all the walks, which would certainly enable you to get to know this great city. If you are unable to physically complete the walks, this book could be used as a reference. However, you choose to use the book, I hope that you find York as endlessly fascinating as I do.

Timeline of York

AD 71	York founded by the Romans. Eboracum is born.
410	The Romans abandon York.
524	Anglo-Saxons drive the British out of York. The city becomes Eoforwic.
868	Vikings capture York and establish control over the area.
954	Vikings expelled from York by Anglo-Saxon King Edgar.
1066	Last Viking invasion defeated by Harold Godwinson.
1068	William the Conqueror builds a castle at York to subdue the population.
1190	Anti-Semitic riots lead to 150 Jews dying in Clifford's Tower.
1291	Work begins on the Gothic Minster.
1300-1400	Powerful guilds become established. Population reaches 10,000.
1455-85	The War of the Roses results in the Duke of York's head being spiked on Micklegate Bar.
1472	Minster completed.
1604	Plague causes 3,512 deaths.
1639	Charles 1 sets up Royal Mint at York and printing press in St William's College to circulate Royal propaganda in dispute with Parliament that leads to the Civil War.
1644	York, a Royalist stronghold, is besieged by Parliamentarians. The city surrenders after the Royalist army is defeated at Marston Moor.
1731-2	The Assembly Rooms are built and York becomes a meeting place for smart Georgian society.

Timeline of York

1745	After the failure of the Jacobite Rebellion against the Hanoverian King George II, public hangings of rebels become popular entertainment on the Knavesmire.
1767	Terry's Confectionary Works established in Clementhorpe.
1838	Rowntree Works founded in Coppergate.
1840	The first journey by rail from York to London.
1942	Baedeker raids by German bombers damage several buildings. The Minster escapes.
1963	York University founded.
1976-81	Archaeologists find remains of Viking York (Yorvik) and the whole world becomes excited. The "dig" attracts royal visitors from Scandinavia.
1984	Lightning strikes the Minster and destroys the roof of the South Transept.
1996	York becomes a unitary authority and expands to take in a number of surrounding villages.

THE WALKS

Walk 1:
Roman Walk

In AD 71 the Romans, stationed at Lincoln, were having trouble with the rebellious northern Celtic tribe, the Brigantes. With approximately 5000 soldiers, Roman General Quintus Petillius Cerialis marched west and established a fort on a patch of land protected by the River Ouse and the River Fosse. Named Eboracum, the place of the Yew trees, the first fort was of earthen ramparts with wooden palisades, which they later replaced with stone between AD 107 and AD 108. As time progressed, a civilian area (colonia) was established on the other side of the River Ouse to service the encampment. It is believed that the colonia was linked to the fortress by a bridge running over the River Ouse to where Tanner Row stands today.

Roman forts were always built to the same plan. The outer walls enclosed a rectangular space of about 50 acres. Inside, a grid of streets and buildings performed the same function from fort to fort. The four corners of the fortress were placed at the points of the compass - north, south, east and west, so on a map of York the fort looks like a distorted diamond shape. Straight main streets ran through the fortress to the four main gateways (portae), which gave access to the main roads outside and correlate with the modern entrances to the city. In time Eboracum became the largest Roman town in the north and the capital of Britannia Inferior. Several Roman emperors visited - Hadrian in 122AD en route to his wall in the north; Septimius Severus arrived in 208AD and used the fortress as his base to try to subdue the Scottish. In AD 237 Eboracum was elevated to the statu s of a colonia, the highest legal status any Roman city could attain, one of only four in Britain. This walk traces the little that is left of both the fortress and the colonia, with an optional extra to visit the site of the Roman cemetery outside the city.

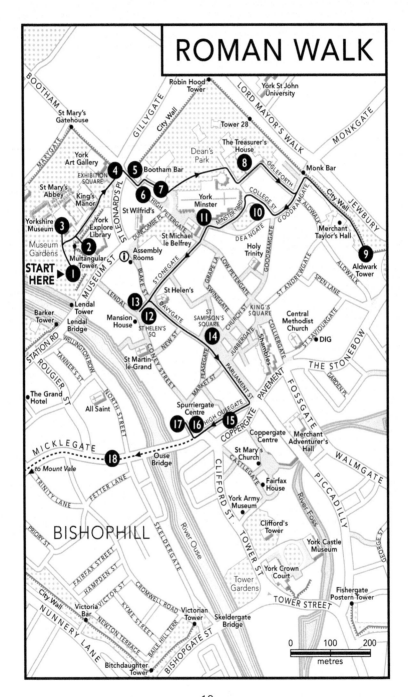

ROMAN WALK

St Mary's Gatehouse

BOOTHAM

MARYGATE

GILLYGATE

Robin Hood Tower

City Wall

York St John University

LORD MAYOR'S WALK

MONKGATE

Tower 28

The Treasurer's House

Dean's Park

York Art Gallery

EXHIBITION SQUARE

4 **5** Bootham Bar

8

OGLEFORTH

Monk Bar

City Wall

JEWBURY

St Mary's Abbey

King's Manor

6 **7**

ST LEONARD'S PL

St Wilfrid's

HIGH PETERGATE

York Minster

COLLEGE ST

GOODRAMGATE

ALDWALK

Merchant Taylor's Hall

Yorkshire Museum

3

York Explore Library

DUNCOMBE PL

MINSTER YARD

11 **10**

DEANGATE

9

Aldwark Tower

Museum Gardens

2

Multangular Tower

MUSEUM ST

Assembly Rooms

STONEGATE

BLAKE ST

Holy Trinity

GRAPE LA

LOW PETERGATE

ST ANDREWGATE

SPEN LANE

ALDWALK

START HERE ▶ **1**

Barker Tower

Lendal Tower

LENDAL

St Helen's

St Michael le Belfrey

ST HELEN'S SQ

SWINEGATE

CHURCH ST

KING'S SQUARE

Central Methodist Church

ST SAVIOURGATE

Lendal Bridge

Mansion House

13

12

DAVYGATE

NEW ST

ST SAMPSON'S SQUARE

14

JUBBERGATE

Shambles

COLLIERGATE

GARDEN PL

DIG

STATION RD

ROUGIER ST

TANNER'S ST

WELLINGTON ROW

CONEY STREET

St Martin-le-Grand

PARLIAMENT ST

PAVEMENT

FOSSGATE

THE STONEBOW

The Grand Hotel

All Saint

NORTH STREET

FEASEGATE

MARKET ST

Spurriergate Centre

17 **16**

HIGH OUSEGATE

15

COPPERGATE

Coppergate Centre

Merchant Adventurer's Hall

WALMGATE

PICCADILLY

MICKLEGATE

18

Ouse Bridge

CLIFFORD ST.

St Mary's Church

CASTLEGATE

Fairfax House

River Foss

GEORGE ST

to Mount Vale

TRINITY LANE

FETTER LANE

York Army Museum

BISHOPHILL

PRIORY ST

FAIRFAX STREET

SKELDERGATE

River Ouse

TOWER ST.

Clifford's Tower

York Castle Museum

HAMPDEN STREET

VICTOR STREET

CROMWELL ROAD

Victorian Tower

Skeldergate Bridge

York Crown Court

Tower Gardens

TOWER STREET

Fishergate Postern Tower

City Wall

Victoria Bar

NEWTON TERRACE

KYME STREET

BAILE HILL TERR.

NUNNERY LANE

Bitchdaughter Tower

BISHOPGATE ST.

0   100   200
metres

10

1. The Museum Gardens - Multangular Tower and fortress wall.

Begin your walk at the Yorkshire Museum Gardens. From the main gates in the city centre, find the wall and tower at the northern end with the colonnaded Yorkshire Museum building on your left. You are now standing in front of the Multangular Tower (or West Angle Tower) and fortress wall.

These are the best remains of the walls of the Roman fort and date from between AD 200 to AD 300. Notice the two fine layers of terracotta bricks in the wall for decoration and structural strength. This section would have once made up the western part of the Roman fort. The original fort of AD 71, built by the Ninth Legion Hispana, would have been made out of timber palisades. The ten-sided brick Multangular Tower was probably built by the Sixth Legion Victrix, which arrived in AD 122 to replace the Ninth.

2. Behind the Multangular Tower.

From the Multangular Tower, walk to the left where you will see a little path through the rockery that leads up through a gap in the wall behind the tower. Walk through the gap to view the tower from the other side with the public library behind you.

From this side you can see that the tower is made of two kinds of masonry. The small bricks in the lower half are Roman, whereas the upper half with the arrow slits was added in the medieval period. The stone coffins at the base of the tower are Roman. Before leaving this area you can explore the remains of the Roman walls that run to right of the Multangular Tower. The walls with the remnants of terracotta bricks are the Roman ones. The higher ones are medieval. If you walk to the end you will come to another tower, the Anglian Tower, built by the Anglo-Saxons, evidence that the walls were altered and added to after the Romans left in AD 410.

3. Optional visit to Yorkshire Museum.

If you cannot wait until the end of the walk, here is your opportunity to visit the Yorkshire Museum that houses various interesting Roman artefacts, mosaics and sarcophogi. Be sure not to miss the life-size statue of Mars that greets you at the entrance. However, it is recommended that you visit at the end of the walk when the exhibits will have more relevance for you.

Opening Times: www.yorkshiremuseum.org.uk

4. Wall Fragments.

Leave the Multangular Tower by the same path that you walked up. Back in the museum gardens you will notice an old building, the King's Manor, to the right of the Yorkshire Museum. Follow the line of the wall that you have just been behind, and this will take you down the side of the King's Manor. As you approach the main road, look to your right.

Here you will find a fragment of the Roman wall and a plaque.

5. Exhibition Square - Bootham Bar.

Walk to your left towards the statue of William Etty on a plinth in the middle of Exhibition Square. Look across the road at Bootham Bar.

This was the site of one of four entrances into the Roman fortress and was called the Porta Principalis Dextra, in other words, "the main gateway on the right". Currently, you can see the remains of the original gateway in the floor of the café to the right of Bootham Bar.

6. High Petergate - Via Principalis.
Walk through Bootham Bar and look down High Petergate.

You are now standing above the original *Via Principalis. The Porta Principalis Dextra* always led to the *Via Principalis*, which in turn always led to the Principia, the headquarters of the fort. The road would have been slightly straighter in Roman times.

7. Precentor's Court - Dean's Park- Principia.
Walk along High Petergate and just before the Hole in the Wall pub on the left, you will find a short alleyway called Little Peculiar Lane. Walk down this alleyway and you will arrive at Precentor's Court. Walk along this street and find the entrance to Dean's Park, the garden of York Minster, on the left. Enter Dean's Park and take a seat.

Imagine that on this site once stood the *Principia* of the fortress, the administrative headquarters. Imagine a range of buildings on each side of a courtyard, including granaries, workshops, a hospital, a barracks and the commanding officer's house (*praetorium*), similar to a splendid townhouse, which would have been used for domestic and business purposes. Remains of the praetorium have been found underneath the Minster. Where the Minster stands today would have been the site of the *basilica*, a great aisled hall.

8. Dean's Park to the Treasurer's House to the Via Decumana.
Leave the garden of Dean's Park by the gate at the opposite end to which you entered. Turn right on the cobbled street and walk past the Treasurer's House. At the end of the Treasurer's House you will come to a street called Chapter House Street.

This small street was the Via Decumana of the fortress. This simply means the east-west orientated road and every Roman fortress had one.

Walk down Chapter House Street to arrive at Ogleforth. Then turn left onto Goodramgate. Next turn left towards Monk Bar. Looking at Monk Bar from inside the city walls, take the steps up onto the city walls on the right-hand side.

9. Monk Bar to Aldwark Tower.

Monk Bar would have been roughly were the north eastern gateway of the fort was. As you walk along the walls, keep looking down into the gardens on your right. After approximately 100 metres you will have walked along the original line of the Roman defensive wall. Notice the medieval Merchant Taylor's Hall. Look down and behind this hall you will see the remains of the eastern corner tower of the Roman fortress.

Aldwark Tower (or East Angle Tower) was not excavated until the 1920s and stands diagonally opposite to the Multangular Tower. It dates from about AD 200, the time of the emperor Septimius Severus.

Now retrace your steps back to Monk Bar.

10. Monk Bar to the Minster.

From Monk Bar walk into the city along Goodramgate and turn right onto College Street with the Minster in front of you. Take the road fork to the left of the Minster (Deangate) past the headquarters of the York Glaziers Trust. Arrive at Minster Yard and notice the statue of the Emperor Constantine.

Constantine's father, Emperor Constantinus, died in Eboracum in AD 306. His son, Constantine was declared emperor by the legionnaires of the fortress that same year. Later in AD 313 Constantine made a declaration that was to change the Western world forever - the Roman Empire was to convert to Christianity.

Look to your right and you will see a huge Roman column.

This is one of sixteen 25 ft columns that once held up the roof of the basilica, the meeting place of the Roman fortress. In 1969, during building work, the column was found in the south transept of the Minster, lying where it had collapsed. It was given by the Dean and Chapter to York Civic Trust which erected it on this site in 1971. York Minster is built on the site of the basilica and the Undercroft Museum of the Minster houses important Roman relics. You can see remnants of the bases of other columns of the basilica, as well as jewellery, tiles, sculptures, Roman wall paintings and even a Roman drain.

Optional Visit: Undercroft Museum of York Minster. (www. yorkminster.org)

11. Minster Yard - Stonegate.

Leave Minster Yard by the small street after the colonnade (Minster Gates). Cross Petergate and directly ahead of you is Stonegate. Walk along Stonegate.

You are now on top of a paved street that was once the Via Praetoria, the way of the Praetorian Guard, the personal guard of the commander of the fortress. This street would have led from the praetoria, the house of the commanding officer, down to the south-west gateway of the fort. Archaeologists have seen the grooves made by the wheels of the ancient chariots in the paving stones below. Try to imagine horse-drawn chariots clattering along the street as you walk to the end!

12. Stonegate to St Helen's Square.

At the end of Stonegate you will arrive at St Helen's Square.

This square is named after the emperor Constantine's mother, who it is believed was influential in converting him to Christianity.

13. Yorkshire Insurance Company, St Helen's Square.

Find the building that once housed the Yorkshire Insurance Company on the right of St Helen's Square. You are now standing on the spot that would have been the main gateway into the fortress - the Porta Praetoria.

This would have been the most spectacular of the four gateways - double-arched and flanked by towers. Remnants of the gateway are to be found in the basement of the building.

Now look across the square at the white and red Mansion House and imagine that it does not exist. Beyond the Mansion House is the River Ouse and in Roman times the river would have been teeming with boats unloading wine and olive oil, then re-loading with sacks of grain from the rich farmland surrounding York. Over the river would have been a bridge that led to the colonia of the fort, where the civilians who served the military encampment lived.

14. St Helen's Square to The Roman Bath Pub.

Leave St Helen's Square by walking back to the church and along Davygate to the right. Walk until the street opens out into St Sampson's Square, where you will find the Roman Bath pub.

In 1930 part of the *caldarium* (steam room) of the Roman bathhouse for the legionnaires was discovered beneath this pub. The bathhouse of Eboracum was huge and occupied the southern corner of the fortress. The bath was not just a place for washing, but for socialising. Evidence of gambling has been found in the form of pottery counters in the silt of the sewers. Gold trinkets in the sewer probably belonged to officers' wives who were allowed to use the baths at the same time as their husbands. Bathing in Roman times involved taking off your clothes and relaxing in the warm *tepidarium*. Afterwards, bathers went into the hot room called the *caldarium* where the steam would make them sweat. In the next room a slave with a bent metal instrument called a *strigil* would scrape the dirt and sweat off their bodies. They would then plunge into the cold bath called the *frigidarium*. Baths were luxurious places decorated with mirrors and mosaic tiled floors.

Optional Visit - The Roman Bath Pub.

In the cellar of the pub, you can see the excavated remains of part of the *frigidarium* and *caldarium* with its tiled floor.

15. Roman Bath Pub to High Ousegate.

From St Sampson's Square walk along Parliament Street towards the traffic lights at the bottom of the road. Take the first right (High Ousegate) and walk along until you arrive at the corner of Nessgate. Find the inscription stone in the sandstone coloured building on your left.

This is a copy of an inscribed stone found during the building's construction in 1843. The original is in the collection of the Yorkshire Museum. It describes the restoration of a temple dedicated to one of the many Roman gods, Hercules. References to the Roman name for York are rare in the city's archaeology and this is the only object in the museum's collection that records the word 'Eboracum'. The inscription gives the settlement its official designation as a colonia, the highest form of self-governing city in the Roman Empire. **Look towards Coney Street on your right.** Archaeologists have found the charred remains of a warehouse here that may have burnt down in the 1st century, suggesting that a fire may have swept through this area of the colonia. This section was called the *vicus* where food and supplies would have been stored in warehouses after being unloaded from the River Ouse.

16. Nessgate to Spurriergate Centre.

With your back to the inscribed stone, cross the road to the Spurriergate Centre (formerly St Michael's church).

The church was built upon what was once the Temple of Hercules. The Romans were pagans and worshipped a range of gods. Altars to Mars, Hercules, Jupiter and Fortune have been found. The most popular deities of Eboracum were the Mother Goddess and the cult of Mithras.

17. Spurriergate Centre to Church Street.

From the Spurriergate Centre walk towards the River Ouse and take the first right onto Church Street.

In 1972 a Roman sewer was discovered on the north side of this street. It was used to carry waste water from the baths and latrines. It extended forty-four metres and was tall enough to allow slaves to crawl along to clean it. Analysed sewage shows that the residents of Eboracum were riddled with worms and bowel parasites. Analysis of organic matter suggests that they used marine sponges for washing and that these were for communal use, not individual! You can now choose to end your walk here or to make the optional extension.

18. Optional Extension - The Mount.

At the Spurriergate Centre walk over Bridge Street and the River Ouse. Keep straight ahead and walk along Micklegate.

Between numbers 1-9 Micklegate a huge public building with a 13ft wall has been excavated, possibly a Roman bath in what was once the *colonia*.

Continue walking beyond Micklegate Bar to Blossom Street. Continue for 0.6 miles until you arrive at the street called The Mount. Turn right at Dalton Terrace and then turn left onto Driffield Terrace.

A Roman cemetery was excavated in this area in 2004. 96 burials were found and the evidence suggests that they were gladiators who had been decapitated. The burials date from the second and third centuries and perhaps possibly the fourth. Underneath numbers 3-6 Driffield Terrace 82 inhumations and 14 cremations where found. All were young adult males. The heads of several individuals had been placed in unusual positions in the graves, such as near the feet. The majority of the blows to the neck were from behind and delivered soon after death. However, in some instances the cut was not complete and the head remained attached to the body. Some suggest that the practise of cutting off heads was so that the head could not return to haunt the living. There was also evidence of a large carnivore bite mark on one individual - either from a bear, a lion or a tiger! Many skeletons had fractures, indicating that they had taken a savage beating or had been tortured before death. There was some debate as to whether the skeletons were of gladiators, soldiers, criminals, or slaves. Experts have concluded that they were gladiators. However, to this day no-one knows the location of the amphitheatre that they would have died in.

19. Trentholme Drive.

Look to your left and turn down Trentholme Drive.

Excavations here in the 1950s found a substantial Roman cemetery. Usually Roman burials are in wooden coffins. Here 90 stone coffins and 25 lead coffins were found. Females were often buried wearing their jewellery and there were many fine jet items - bracelets, rings, hair pins and medallions with figures in relief. Skeletal evidence shows that many of the inhabitants had lived a life of violence. Twenty-one healed upper and lower limb fractures were found, including a fractured thigh bone. Several more thigh bones displayed depressions consistent with sword cuts.

20. 147 Mount Vale.

Return to Tadcaster Road and find 147 Mount Vale.

Excavations at 147 Mount Vale in 1918 unearthed 75 Roman skeletons in an area which would have been an extension to the Roman burial ground further along this area. Very few grave goods suggest that the people were of low social status. Well done. You have completed your walk.

Christian Walk: Part 1

In AD 313 Constantine the Great converted to Christianity, paving the way for the Roman Empire to follow suit. Subsequently, the once pagan Anglo-Saxons and pagan Vikings who had fought over York for several centuries, each eventually converted to Christianity themselves. Consequently, traces of their Christian devotion can still be found in some of the churches of York. The Minster was built on the site of an Anglo-Saxon church and its presence has made York the ecclesiastical second city of England to this day. By the medieval period the Christian religion dominated every one's life. Churches, chapels, friaries, priories and chantries were everywhere. The times of masses dictated when markets could be opened and the city gates closed. The church owned land and influenced politics, commerce and culture. People lived by the Seven Acts of Mercy, which obliged them to provide food, drink, clothing and hospitality to those in need. If you complied, you would go to heaven. If you erred, you would go to hell. Like everywhere else, York was firmly under religious rule with forty churches within the city walls, until Henry VIII began to dissolve the monasteries in 1536. There are so many churches in York that this walking tour has been divided into two parts to allow you to enjoy learning about York's rich Christian heritage little by little. A good tip is to walk around the exterior of a church first to see if you can spot the layers of history in the stonework, then venture inside, if it is open.

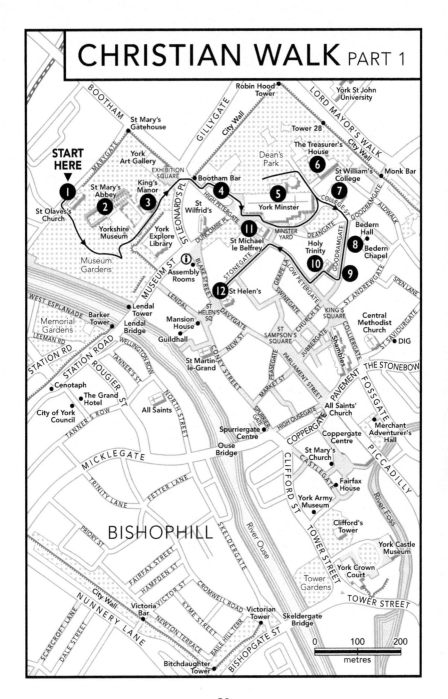

CHRISTIAN WALK PART 1

Start:	St Olave's Church, Marygate next to The Yorkshire Museum Gardens
End:	Davygate Burial Ground

1. St Olave's Church, Marygate.

Begin your walk at St Olave's Church, Marygate on the north-western edge of the Yorkshire Museum Gardens.

This earliest church on this site was probably a chapel belonging to the Anglo-Saxon Earls of Northumbria. Nothing remains of this building above ground. Evidence suggests that later Christianised Vikings took over the church. The name itself, St Olave, bears witness to this as Olaf was the patron saint of Norway. Grave slabs of Viking design were found in neighbouring St Mary's Abbey and most certainly came from this church. The church is listed in the Anglo-Saxon Chronicle in 1055 as the burial place of Siward, the earl of Northumbria, showing that by this time it was back in Anglo-Saxon hands. After the Norman Conquest, it became the church of the Benedictine order in York. In 1644 during the Siege of York in the Civil War a gun platform was placed on top of the church. Inside you can see St Olaf featured in the East Window.

2. St Mary's Abbey, Yorkshire Museum Gardens.

Leave St Olave's and enter the gates of the Yorkshire Museum Gardens to the right of the church. As you walk along the path, look left to where you will see the remains of St Mary's Abbey.

After 1066 the church of St Olave's and surrounding land was given to Alan of Brittany. In turn he granted four acres of land to Benedictine monks from Whitby and Lastingham. In an attempt to re-establish the monastic tradition in the north of England, they founded an abbey and in 1089 it was dedicated to St. Mary. This was to become one of the greatest abbeys in medieval England. Look to your right and you will see an impressive building that now hosts special events. This is the 14th century hospitium of the abbey - a guest house for lower rank visitors and a warehouse for goods, conveniently located next to the river. Its name derives from "hospitality", not "hospital." In the grounds of the abbey there would also have been a brew-house, stables, a mill and near the main gate, a boarding school for 50 pupils.

3. The King's Manor.

Proceed through the museum gardens, past the colonnaded Yorkshire Museum. To the right of the museum you will see another building set back, with the city walls to its right. This is the King's Manor. Walk along the side of the King's Manor, then turn left into the gates of King's Manor.

This impressive building was once the seat of the Abbot of St Mary's. However, in 1536 it was confiscated by Henry VIII and became his headquarters whenever he was in the north, hence the name. Later it became the headquarters of the Council of the North, a body Henry VIII set up to give him more control over the rebellious north. Later it became a school for the blind and is currently leased by the University of York. Several rooms are open to the public and there is a pleasant café, where the councillors once met, open during the week.

4. King's Manor to York Minster.

Leave King's Manor in the direction of the statue of William Etty on the plinth at Exhibition Square. Cross the road and head through Bootham Bar. Walk down High Petergate and notice the little snickelway just before the Hole in the Wall pub (Little Peculiar Lane). Enter the snickelway to emerge at Precentor's Court.

The precentor is the church official in charge of the music at the Minster. Many of the buildings on this street would have been connected to the Minster in one way or another. Walk along Precentor's Court until you arrive at western end of York Minster.

York Minster stands near the
site of an Anglo-Saxon church.
Later a more impressive Minster
was built, which burnt down
during the fighting between
the Normans and the Anglo-
Saxons in 1068. The Normans
prevailed and appointed Thomas
of Bayeaux (1070-1100) to be the
new Archbishop. He rebuilt the
cathedral only to see it ransacked
again in 1075 by the final Viking
raid on the city. At this point
Archbishop Thomas decided to
find a new location for the Minster
and chose the site of the ancient

Roman principia. Re-using much of the stone from the principia,
the huge white edifice would have been visible for miles around,
towering above other buildings, testament to might of the new
Norman rulers. It had taken a mere 20 years to build.

Archbishop Walter Gray (1215-1255) noticed that in France and
Canterbury new Gothic cathedrals were being built. Although the new
Minster would take 250 years to build, Walter Gray oversaw the building
of the south transept with its beautiful rose (or wheel) window, which
commemorates the marriage of Elizabeth of York to Henry VII in 1485.

**Walk around the exterior of the Minster in an anti-clockwise
direction.**

Stand in Minster Yard and admire the beautiful, delicate tracery of the
rose (or wheel) window.

**On the eastern side of the Minster, facing St William's College,
you will find the Great East Window, popularly known as the "Heart
of Yorkshire".**

This is the largest expanse of Medieval glass anywhere in the country.
God is at the top, looking down on everyone below.

**Walk towards the cobbled lane on your right and enter the garden
behind the Minster (Dean's Park) where you can view the rest of the
building.**

On this side you will notice the Five Sisters Window - five tall lancets in Early English style. This window was removed for safety during the First World War and restored in 1924.

Optional Visit: www.yorkminster.org

6. Dean's Park to the Treasurer's House.

Dean's Park is named after the Dean, who is the chief administrator of the archbishopric. With your back to the Minster you will notice a building tucked away at the right of park. This is the Minster Library, housed in the former palace of the Archbishop, which holds 300,000 objects including 90,000 volumes dating back to 1470. You can access the collection by appointment.

Leave Dean's Park through the same gates that you entered by and now you will find yourself in front of the Treasurer's House.

Once the living quarters of the treasurer of the Minster, who controlled the finances, in the nineteenth century the building was bought by Frank Green, the heir of a wealthy Yorkshire industrialist who lavishly renovated it.

Optional Visit: The Treasurer's House www.nationaltrust.org.uk

7. St William's College.

From the Treasurer's House walk towards the Minster along the cobbled lane and turn right onto College Street. On the left you will find St William's College.

In 1462 this timber-framed building became the home of the 1461 of the Vicars- Choral of York Minster, also known as chantry priests, who were paid to pray for the souls of the dead.

8. Bedern Chapel.

From the National Trust shop next to St William's College, turn right and walk along Goodramgate towards the centre of the city. Almost immediately on the left you will see an arched alleyway. Enter the alleyway to find Bedern Chapel on the right.

Bedern Chapel was the chapel of the Vicars Choral. Nearby is Bedern Hall where they were required to live together from 1250. However, due to their violent nocturnal habits (such as hitting someone over the head with the blunt end of an axe), they were moved to St William's College, nearer to the Minster, so that a closer eye could be kept on them.

9. Goodramgate to Our Lady's Row.

Return to Goodramgate and walk towards the city centre until you come upon a row of painted buildings with over-hanging upper stories where you will find a plaque giving information about Our Lady's Row.

Built in the early 14th century, these houses are the earliest example in England of an upper floor projecting beyond the lower floor. Their name refers to the Virgin Mary because they were built as accommodation for Holy Trinity Church, which lies behind the row. A priest would have lived here, employed to say masses for the people of York and the rent from the rest of the accommodation would have helped to fund the church. In the mid-15th century a religious recluse lived here. In 1827 a move to demolish the row was fortunately overturned, thereby saving York's oldest buildings.

10. Holy Trinity Church, Goodramgate.

Next to Our Lady's Row, towards the centre of the city is a brick archway. Turn right through the archway where you will find Holy Trinity Church, hidden away from the hustle and bustle of the shopping thoroughfare in its own secluded churchyard.

Holy Trinity dates largely from the 15th century, but has features from the 12th century to the 19th century. The east window dates from the 1470s and was donated by the rector of the church, Reverend John Walker. The box pews are Jacobean and are the only surviving examples in York. The church contains an inner chapel which was once isolated from the main church and may have allowed lepers to see the services through a hagioscope (squint hole) in the wall. Alternatively, the hagioscope may have allowed the chantry priest to say mass in unison with the priest at the altar. See if you can find the rare "piscina", a hole in the wall that was used for washing the chalice after communion. As there is no gas, electricity or running water, a unique atmosphere exists in the church. In 2019 it featured in the BBC series "Gentleman Jack" due to a ceremony with Anne Lister and Ann Walker. A plaque now commemorates this event.

11. Holy Trinity, Goodramgate to St Michael-Le- Belfrey.

Leave Holy Trinity churchyard by the alleyway to the left of the church called Hornpot Lane to arrive at Low Petergate. Turn right and walk to the end of the street where you will find the St Michael-Le- Belfrey church.

This church takes its name from the belfry in the south transept of the Minster and was the church of the lay people who lived around the Minster. Originally it was one of York's wealthiest parishes. However, the original church of 1294 was completely rebuilt between 1525 and 1536 due to disrepair. The stained glass in the east window survives from the 14th century, which depicts the martyrdom of Thomas Becket, a rare survival as Henry VIII tried to erase all mention of him during the Dissolution of the Monasteries. The lantern tower replaced the bell turret in 1848. Guy Fawkes was christened here on 16th April 1570.

12. St Michael-Le Belfrey to St Helen, Stonegate.

Leave St Michael-Le-Belfrey and walk along Low Petergate towards the city centre. Turn left when you arrive at Stonegate. Walk along Stonegate until you arrive at the church of St Helen at the end.

St Helen's is dedicated to the mother of Constantine the Great, the first Roman Emperor to legalise Christian worship in 313AD. St Helen is believed to have encouraged his conversion to Christianity. The first church on the site dates from before the Norman Conquest and was built of wood. The font is 12th century. By the 13th century, the church was used by the city's glassmakers, many of whom worked in Stonegate. St Helen appears in the stained glass. Look out for the coat of arms of "The Worshipful Company of Glaziers" in one of the windows. The church was saved from demolition in 1551 by a public outcry. The lantern tower replaced the bell turret in 1814. Outside, in what is now St Helen's Square, there would once have been the graveyard of the church. By 1703 the graveyard was preventing the gentry from having easy access to the new and elegant Assembly Rooms and so it was bought by the City Corporation. A new burial plot was created on Davygate, which is still there to this day. In 1745 the square was paved over.

Walk along Davygate towards the centre of the city and St Sampson's Square and Parliament Street. Find the eerie burial ground set back from the shopping thoroughfare. Here ends your walk. Well done!

Christian Walk: Part 2

In Medieval times there were forty parish churches within the city walls, not including the Minster and St Mary's Abbey. Today approximately twenty remain, if you count the fact that one is now a pub. Part 2 of Christian York takes in the remaining churches and any other religious buildings of historic interest found along the way. York is home to 60 percent of the historic stained glass in the country, so be sure not to miss these amazing works of art on your tour. When the writer Daniel Defoe made a tour of Great Britain in 1720, he wrote of York, "there are very neat churches here besides the cathedral, and were not the minster standing, like the Capitol in the middle of the city of Rome, some of these would pass for extraordinary..." This walk takes in the majority of the remaining religious buildings that are of historical and artistic interest.

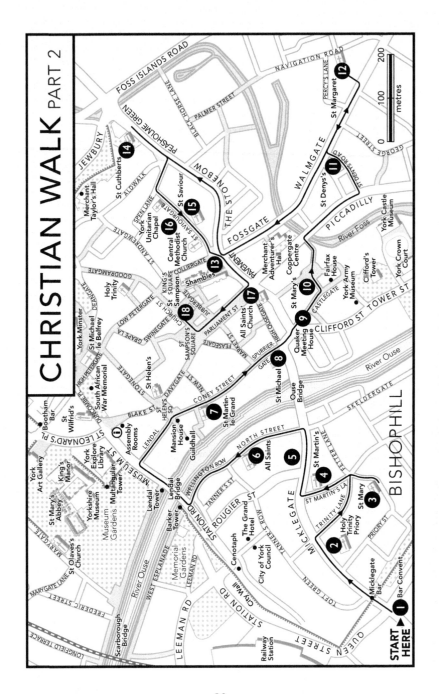

Start: Bar Convent, Nunnery Lane
End: St Sampson, Church Lane

1. Bar Convent, Nunnery Lane.

Begin your walk just outside the city walls at Micklegate Bar. Here you will find the Bar Convent.

Bar Convent is the oldest living convent in England, founded in 1686 to follow the teachings of its founder, Mary Ward (1585-1645), who based her ideas on the Society of Jesus. Mary and many of the future abbesses lived through long periods of fierce persecution of Catholics and this is why the Bar Convent could easily be mistaken for a row of elegant townhouses, as the nuns had to hide in plain sight. Inside the Convent is a spectacular domed chapel, that was once a secret, but is now open to all worshippers. Inside the chapel you can see the priest hole, said to be a secret tunnel leading to a building on the opposite side of the street. The convent also houses a more poignant relic - the embalmed hand of Margaret Clitherow, martyred in 1586. The separate exhibition is open Monday to Saturday from 10am to 5pm (admission charge). The lovely café is good place to gather your energies before you begin your walk.

Optional Visit: Bar Convent www.bar-convent.org.uk

2. Holy Trinity, Micklegate.

Now enter the city through Micklegate Bar and walk on the right-hand side of the road. Pass over Priory Street and you will arrive at Holy Trinity Church on the right.

This church is the only surviving building from what was once a seven-acre monastic complex belonging to the Benedictine order who came to York from France in the 11th century. The other monastic buildings did not survive Henry VIII's Dissolution of the Monasteries (1536-1541), but the church was allowed to continue as a parish church. The current church is on the site of an earlier church that is mentioned in the Domesday book of 1086. Inside the pillars date from the 13th century. The nave is all that remains of the original monastery church.

3. St Mary, Bishophill.

Return to Micklegate and continue walking towards the city centre. Turn right onto Trinity Lane. When you arrive at a junction of roads, turn right onto Bishophill Jr and find St Mary, Bishophill.

This is the oldest surviving church within the city walls and pieces of Roman tilework can be found in the tower. Some scholars believe that it was built in the 8th century; others that it could have been the seat of the Bishop of York in AD 314. The tower is from the late Anglo-Saxon period. Inside you can find a Viking age stone cross fragment that dates to the 10th century. Much of the present church was built from the 12th century throughout the medieval period. It now hosts both a Greek Orthodox and a Russian Orthodox congregation.

4. St Martin-Cum-Gregory, St Martin's Lane.

Return to the junction and instead of going back along Trinity Street, walk down the street that runs parallel to it, St Martin's Lane. St Martin-cum-Gregory is also known as St Martin's Church or the Stained Glass Centre.

This church was mentioned in the 11th century Domesday Book, but much of the building is 14th and 15th century. The tower plinth is made from stone pillaged from the Roman Temple of Mithras. The tower was built in 1844. In 2008 the Stained Glass Centre was established. Aptly, three of the country's leading glaziers are buried here - William Peckitt (1731-1795); his wife and assistant Mary Peckitt and Henry Gyles (1645-1709). Mary Peckitt made a memorial window to her husband that can be admired inside.

5. St John, Micklegate.

Return to Micklegate and walk towards the city centre. On the left you will find St John, Micklegate, which is now a pub.

The base of the tower dates from the 12th century. However, the rest was blown down in a storm in 1551. Most of the current building dates from the 15th century and was restored in 1850. In 1934 the church was closed and its treasures distributed elsewhere. Glass from here is now in the Minster. York Civic Trust saved it from demolition and it became the York Institute of Advanced Architectural Studies, then in the 1960s it became an arts centre run by the University of York.

6. All Saints, North Street.

Now continue to walk towards the city centre and take an immediate left into North Street. Walk along North Street until you arrive at All Saints Church.

The first reference to a church here is in 1089. Notice the properties to the left of the church. This row is called All Saints Cottages and dates from the 15th century. It was a chantry and would have housed men paid to say masses for the souls of their patrons. Inside the church houses some of the finest medieval stained glass in Europe, including the aisle window which shows the Six Corporal Acts of Mercy. In contrast the Doom Window (1410) depicts your final fifteen days before the Day of Judgement. On a cheerier note, try to find the figure in the 14th century south aisle window wearing glasses. This is one of the earliest-known depictions of spectacles.

7. St Martin-le-Grand, Coney Street.

Now continue along North Street in the same direction that you entered and head for Lendal Bridge. Climb the stone staircase, pass over the bridge and take the first right onto Lendal. Ignore St Helen's Square and proceed straight ahead along Coney Street. On your right you will arrive at St Martin-le-Grand.

While this church still holds services, it is also a shrine to all those who lost their lives in the two World Wars due to bombing of the site during the Baedecker Raids, which targeted locations of cultural significance. The clock (1778) was bombed to the ground in 1942, but fortunately the figure of the "Little Admiral" could be saved. Both the clock and the "admiral" were restored in 2013. The church dates from the 11th century and grew in importance when the nearby Mansion House was built in 1703 for the Lord Mayor, leading it to become the official civic church. The window in the south aisle (1477) was removed for safety during World War Two and was later restored by architect George Pace. It shows scenes from the life of St Martin of Tours who made the Devil carry his prayer book. Inside, a unique mechanical pipe organ was a gift from the German government. The tragically martyred Margaret Clitherow was baptised here in about 1553.

8. St Michael, Spurriergate (The Spurriergate Centre).

Back on Coney Street continue ahead in the same direction that you arrived, until the street becomes Spurriergate, where you will find St Michael (Spurrriergate Centre) at the end on the right-hand side.

Dating from the Norman period circa 1088, St Michael stands on the site of the Roman Temple of Hercules. It was decommissioned as a church in 1980 and is now a thriving Christian Centre offering refreshment, counselling and occasional band practice facilities. Inside, the pillars are 12th century and it has a full set of bells which are rung frequently. The tenor bell (1466) is the only surviving medieval bell from York Minster.

9. Quaker Meeting House, Friargate.

Return to Spurriergate and walk towards the busy junction of streets. Ignore the traffic lights and stay on the pedestrianised walkway. Walk beyond Nessgate and cross over the pedestrian crossing onto Coppergate. Then turn right onto Castlegate. As you walk along Castlegate, notice the street on the right called Friargate.

Here is Friargate Quaker Meeting House, just one of York's many non-conformist gathering places. The façade is from 1885, although the interior dates to 1815. Quakers have no ministers; they meet in silence until a member of the congregation feels moved to speak. The philanthropy of the Quakers has had a huge impact on the history of York. For more information see the Chocolate Walk.

10. St Mary, Castlegate.

Return to Castlegate and proceed along the street where you will find St Mary's.

There has been a church on this site since the 11th century, but most of what can be seen is 15th century. A dedication stone records that it was founded by [Ef]rard, Grim and AEse. Its proximity to the Coppergate Viking site suggests that it was founded by the Viking community. Under the chancel arch, a recycled Roman column capital and fragments of three column drums have been found. The steeple is the tallest in York at 154 feet. It was decommissioned in 1958 and is used for various temporary exhibitions, with limited opening times.

11. St Denys's, Walmgate.

Leave St Mary's by entering the Coppergate Shopping Complex and taking the car park tunnel exit in the right-hand corner out onto Piccadilly. On Piccadilly turn right. Ignore Dennis Street on your left and carry on until the next street, St Denys Road. Walk along this street until you find the church.

The church has ancient origins with evidence of previous Roman, Viking and Anglo-Saxon buildings on the site. A third century Roman altar dedicated to the Roman God Arciaco was unearthed from beneath a church pillar in 1846. (Now in the Yorkshire Museum). An Anglo-Danish tombstone was also found. The church had a close connection with the Percy family, the earls of Northumberland whose townhouse, Percy Inn, stood opposite. Several are buried here, including the 3rd Earl, Henry Percy, who died at the battle of Towton in 1461. The east window is from the 15th century and depicts St Denys or Dionysius holding his own severed head because he was martyred in Paris. There are also two reset 12th century roundels, the oldest stained glass in the city. This church has been dubbed "the unlucky church" due to the spire being struck down by a cannon ball in the Siege of York. In 1700 it was struck by lightning and then in the 18th century part of it subsided when the King's Fishpool was drained. A collapsed sewer took out another part of the building. It is quite miraculous that it is still here at all!

12. St Margaret, Walmgate (Optional Detour)

Leave St Denys Church and turn onto Walmgate. Walk to the right and you will arrive at the decommissioned church of St Margaret, which is now the National Centre for Early Music. Access to the church is limited. The best way to see it is by enjoying a concert there with its unique atmosphere.

Founded in the 11th century, it was substantially rebuilt in the Middle Ages, then in the 17th century after the Civil War, and finally by the Victorians. It fell into disuse in the 1960s. Originally there were six churches in the Walmgate area, now there are only two.

13. St Crux Church Hall

From St Denys's on Walmgate, walk to the left towards the centre of the city. At the end of Walmgate cross over the road to St Crux Church Hall.

This church hall is all that is left of what was once considered one of the most wonderful churches of York. St Crux, Pavement would have stood where the current Marks and Spencer building is. The dynamiting of the Italianate tower and cupola in 1887 has been described as "one of the most depressing acts of Victorian civic vandalism to be visited on any city" by York historian, Paul Chrystal. St Crux church dated back to the 15th century and some suspect its destruction was due to xenophobia towards Italianate features, rather than to its health and safety issues. The brick Italianate tower is rumoured to have been designed by Sir Christopher Wren in 1697. You can enjoy an eerie atmosphere in the church hall which is adorned with re-housed grave tablets. You can also pick up a very reasonable cup of tea and sandwich, if it is open.

14. St Cuthbert, Peaseholme Green

Leave St Crux Church Hall in the direction of Pavement, away from the Shambles. With your back to the hall on Pavement, turn left and head down Stonebow, which leads into Peaseholme Green.

This church is situated at what was once the north east corner of the Roman fortress and the east wall of the church is built from Roman masonry. It is from here that we have evidence that the Ninth Legion Hispana was in York as a tile stamped with the inscription LEG IX HISP has been found. The existing building dates back to 1430 when the original was restored and rebuilt by William de Bowes, Lord Mayor of York, who lived at the Black Swan Inn on the opposite side of the road. The church is now a centre for prayer and mission.

15. St Saviour, Saviourgate

Return to Peaseholme Green and retrace your steps towards the city centre. Turn right onto St Saviour's Place. Then turn left into St Saviourgate and the church will be on the left.

There has been a church here since the 11th century, although much of the present building dates from the 15th century. The church was made redundant in 1954 and the medieval glass and fitments dispersed throughout the city. In 1990 York Archaeological Trust set up its resource centre there.

16. York Unitarian Chapel and Central Methodist Church

Also on St Saviourgate you will find two buildings which reflect Non-conformism in York. To the right of St Saviour is York Unitarian Chapel.

Unitarianism began after the restoration of Charles II in 1660. Puritans wanted to worship without ornate rituals and the 1689 Act of Toleration allowed them to exist. Lady Hewley, along with several others, built a brick meeting house in 1693. Unusually, it is built in the shape of Greek cross, unique among English churches.

To the left of St Saviour is the Central Methodist Church.

Built in 1840 to mark 100 years of Methodism, the chapel was originally known as the Centenary Chapel. Constructed on a grand scale, the main hall seats 1,500 people.

17. All Saints, Pavement.

Walk back towards St Crux Church Hall. Walk beyond the Shambles and Marks and Spencer. Ahead you should be able to spot All Saints, Pavement due to its beautiful, distinctive lantern tower.

The lantern tower of All Saints, Pavement is not simply decorative. Dating from around 1400, the octagonal tower would have held a beaming, burning light to guide travellers to York through the wolf-infested Forest of Galtres, which once surrounded York. After the First World War it was restored and is now lit every evening as a memorial to all those who died. Inside All Saints, there are works of art which have been salvaged from St Saviour and St Crux. The west window from St Saviour dates from 1370 and shows scenes from the life of Christ. Another window is dedicated to Mary Craven (1826-1900), pioneering York confectioner. Inside there are many interesting relics and a beautiful new stained glass window to commemorate the soldiers who died in Afghanistan. A church has stood here since AD 685 and the current building dates from the 14th and 15th century. Inside see if you can find the stone coffin of a Viking child and the replica sword of Thomas Percy, beheaded on Pavement for defying Elizabeth 1.

Walk up Pavement, the wide esplanade in front of Marks and Spencer and turn right into Church Street.

St Sampson is now a centre for the over 60's. The church was built into the wall of the old Roman fortress. There are some Norman remnants, but it appears to have been extensively re-built in the 1400s. Numbers 12 - 15 Newgate are the surviving houses of a row of up to ten chantry houses that the church was allowed to build in 1336. In 1394 Richard II gave the church to the Vicars Choral of York Minster, who owned it until 1936. During the Civil War it was badly damaged by cannon fire and later sacked by Parliamentarian forces. In 1844 it was damaged by fire. In 1848 it was pulled down and a new church was built. Well done. You have completed your walk.

Norman Walk

The Normans invaded Britain in 1066 and according to the chronicler
Orderic Vitalis, York was "seething with discontent". At this time York
would have been a city with Viking heritage, controlled by Anglo-
Saxons. The king of the Normans, William the Conqueror, was
determined to stamp his authority on York and began by building a
wooden castle in 1068 on the site of what is now Clifford's Tower.
That same year the population rebelled and in 1069 William decided
to build a second castle on the western bank of the River Ouse,
now called Baile Hill. The two castles were designed to control river
access to the city by threading a chain between them preventing
passage along the Ouse. In 1070 King Swein of Denmark's warriors
sailed up the River Humber and banded together with the powerful
Anglo-Saxon nobles to attack the Norman garrison. In a defensive
measure to prevent their enemies sheltering in the city, the Normans
set fire to it. The blaze spread and much of it was destroyed,
including the fledgling Minster. Upon hearing of his garrison's defeat
in York, William rushed to the north, swearing an ominous oath:
"By the splendour of God, I will avenge myself on the north." After
bribing the Danes to leave the city, he advanced on York without
opposition. With his two castles repaired, he used the city as a base
to remorselessly and relentlessly lay waste to the region in what has
become known as the "Harrying of the North". Estimates suggest
100,000 people died from violence and famine. It took several
generations to recover. William stayed until Christmas 1069 and
by 1072 both his castles were reconstructed. In 1190 the wooden
keep was set on fire during the infamous massacre of the Jewish
population of York. In 1244 Henry III had the tower rebuilt in stone.

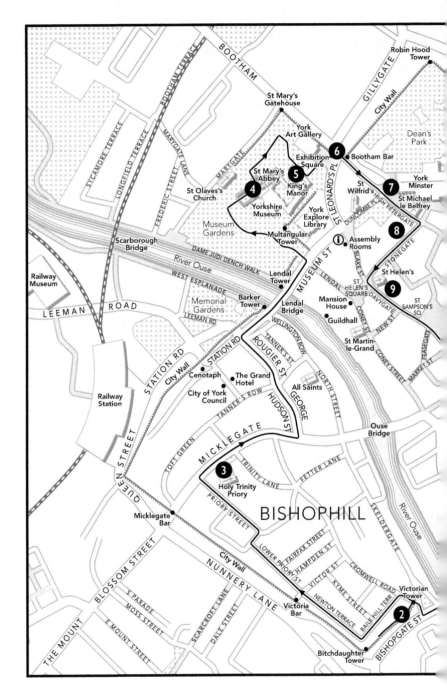

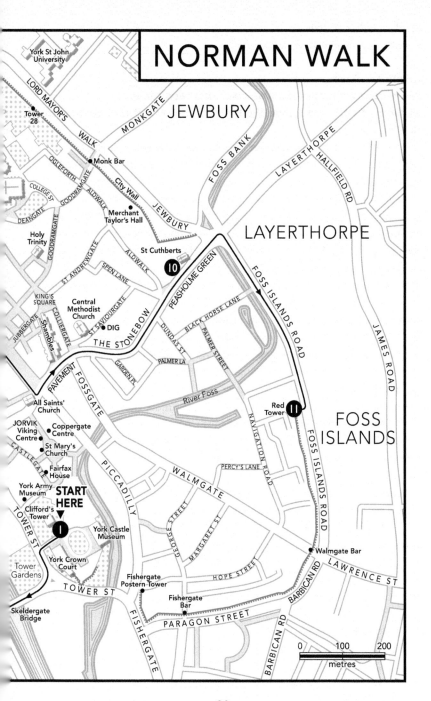

NORMAN WALK

York St John University

Tower 28

LORD MAYOR'S WALK

MONKGATE

JEWBURY

LAYERTHORPE

HALLFIELD RD

Monk Bar

City Wall

OGLEFORTH

COLLEGE ST

GOODRAMGATE

ALDWALK

DEANGATE

Merchant Taylor's Hall

FOSS BANK

JEWBURY

Holy Trinity

St Cuthberts

10

LAYERTHORPE

ST ANDREWGATE

ALDWALK

SPEN LANE

PEASHOLME GREEN

KING'S SQUARE

COLLIERGATE

Central Methodist Church

ST SAVIOURGATE

DIG

FOSS ISLANDS ROAD

JUBBERGATE

Shambles

THE STONEBOW

DUNDAS ST

BLACK HORSE LANE

PALMER STREET

JAMES ROAD

GARDEN PL

PALMER LA

PAVEMENT

All Saints' Church

FOSSGATE

River Foss

Red Tower

11

FOSS ISLANDS

JORVIK Viking Centre

Coppergate Centre

St Mary's Church

Fairfax House

PICCADILLY

WALMGATE

PERCY'S LANE

NAVIGATION ROAD

CASTLEGATE

York Army Museum

START HERE ▼

Clifford's Tower

1

York Castle Museum

GEORGE STREET

MARGARET ST

FOSS ISLANDS ROAD

TOWER ST

Tower Gardens

York Crown Court

HOPE STREET

Walmgate Bar

LAWRENCE ST

BARBICAN RD

Fishergate Postern Tower

Fishergate Bar

BARBICAN RD

Skeldergate Bridge

FISHERGATE

PARAGON STREET

| 0 | 100 | 200 |

metres

39

Start: Clifford's Tower

Finish: Red Tower, Foss Islands Road

1. Clifford's Tower

Begin your walk at Clifford's Tower, perhaps the most iconic emblem of York, alongside the Minster, also affectionately known as the "minced pie".

As you look at the stone tower of the castle complex, imagine how it would have looked in Norman times. Originally the tower would have been made of wood and used as a food and weapons store. With either two or three floors, the topmost platform would have housed a look-out and sentry post. Imagine William's personal banner flying from the roof to emphasise his dominion and power. The mound of earth upon which the keep is built was thrown up by Norman soldiers and is called a "motte". It would have been defended by a wooden palisade or fence. The motte and keep would have been protected by an outer bailey, the extent of which is not known. To the right of the tower where the court and museum are today, the inner bailey would have stood. This was effectively a rectangular fortress which housed several buildings - meeting halls, kitchens, a chapel, barracks, stores, stables, forges, workshops and a prison. This was the seat of Norman power where they would have administered justice. Surrounding the motte and inner bailey would have been a broad water-filled moat. The Normans damned the River Foss, diverted it to create the moat and turned it into a large lake known as the King's Fishpool. The tower and the inner bailey would have been connected by a flight of steps where the current steps are. This was called a "flying bridge" and spanned the moat from the bailey bank to the summit of the motte.

Walk to the stepped entrance to the tower where you will find a memorial to the Jewish massacre of 1190.

The Normans invited Jewish people to England to help them finance their interests. By the 12th century resentment against the Jewish community was growing due to the debts that people had incurred to them. Benedict of York was killed by the mob in London. After rioting engulfed Norwich, Stamford and Lincoln, the York mob attempted to burned down Benedict's house, killing his widow and children. The rioters were egged on by the local gentry including Richard Malebisse who saw the riots as an opportunity to wipe out their extensive debts. 150 Jewish people fled to York Castle and sought sanctuary from the constable in the tower. The constable turned against them and a group of knights arrived to lay siege to the tower. With a baying mob outside, the trapped community saw no other option than to commit mass suicide. Among the men, Josce and Rabbi Yomtob killed the wives and children and then set fire to the wooden keep in order to take their own lives. Those who asked for mercy from the mob were refused and were murdered by the rioters. No individuals were ever punished. Instead the city was fined by King Richard.

Optional Visit: Clifford's Tower www.english-heritage.co.uk

2. Clifford's Tower to Baile Hill

Leave Clifford's Tower by Tower Street, walking away from the city centre towards the bridge. At Bishopgate turn right and walk along Skeldergate Bridge. Ahead you will see a small turret that signals the entrance to the city walls. Climb the steps and walk along the walls until you are looking down at the motte of Baile Hill.

Originally the castle of Old Baile was of motte and bailey design, like its counterpart on the other side of the river. A flight of steps would have led up to a wooden structure on the top of the motte, surrounded by a wooden fence. To the north-west lay the rectangular bailey, surrounded by an earth rampart and outer ditch. By 1340 the city wall had been built here, incorporating the ramparts and the ditch. Houses built during the 1880s now cover the rest of Old Baile.

3. Old Baile to Holy Trinity Priory, Micklegate

Return to ground level and walk along Newton Terrace, which leads into Lower Priory Street. Turn right at Bishophill Junior Street, then left onto Priory Street.

Notice that the streets in this area contain the word "priory". This is because in Norman times, this was a 7 acre monastic complex. Benedictine monks came to York from France in the 11th century and created a large monastic complex with a magnificent priory church at its heart.

At the end of Priory Street, turn right onto Micklegate. (Optional detour: the arch of Micklegate Bar is thought to be Norman.) Proceed to the right and find Holy Trinity Church.

The official name of this church is "The Priory Church of the Holy Trinity".

Before the conquest, a Minster stood on this site, complete with canons. Unfortunately, by 1089 they were "almost reduced to nothing". Later the "alien Benedictine" monks arrived, and a Norman monastery church was built here. Within the monastic complex there was a famous chantry chapel under the priory - the chapel of St James's on the Mount. This church is all that survived of the monastic complex due to Henry VIII's Dissolution of the Monasteries (1536-1541) and is built on the part of the site of the chantry chapel. The church was allowed to continue and is the only parish church in York which was once monastic. However, all that survives of the Norman church is the nave, much reduced in size and width over the centuries.

Optional Visit: Inside there are many artefacts and an interesting exhibition on aspects of monastic life.

4. Holy Trinity, Micklegate to St Mary's Abbey

Leave the church and return to Micklegate. With your back to the church, turn right and walk down to the traffic lights. Turn left onto George Hudson Street. This will then become Rougier Street. At the end of Rougier Street, turn right onto the wide main road (Museum Street). Walk up Museum Street until you see the Yorkshire Museum Gardens on your left. Enter the gardens and find the ruins of St Mary's Abbey at the opposite side of the garden.

Benedictine monks competed this abbey in 1088 for Abbot Stephen and a group of monks from Whitby. It was financed by Alan Rufus, relative and friend of William the Conqueror and his son, William II. The walls around it are the best-preserved section of the wall from Norman times. They were built to protect the monks after the townsfolk became disgruntled. A cleric, Simon de Warwich, imposed high taxes on the market outside Bootham and they attacked the abbey. By 1132 a division developed among the brothers and fourteen of them left York to found the stricter Cistercian Fountains Abbey. As the centuries past, the power of the monks increased. They enjoyed substantial privileges, such as exemption from tax and immunity from prosecution. They could inflict punishment at the gallows in Burton Stone Lane and at Garrow Hill. They were able to levy taxes and market tolls on the land that they owned. In 1343 and 1350 the monks were attacked by armed citizens who threatened to crucify them. A compromise was brokered by Edward III in 1354. By 1539 St Mary's was the largest and richest Benedictine establishment in the north of England and one of the largest landholders in Yorkshire with an annual turnover of £2000. In that same year the Abbey surrendered its money and its fifty monks to the Crown. It was then closed and laid waste by Henry VIII.

5. The King's Manor

Walk beyond the colonnaded Yorkshire Museum and next to it, set back you will see the brick-built abbot's house, now known as the King's Manor. Walk down the side of the King's Manor. Reach the main road. Turn left and appreciate the building from the front.

This house was the home of the abbot of St Mary's and is testament to the style and opulence that the monks had achieved since their arrival in 1088. The current house dates from 1483 and survives as the "King's Manor" because it became the seat of the Council of the North in 1539, the King's Council, set up by Henry VIII to keep a closer eye on the north.

6. Exhibition Square to Bootham Bar

Leave the King's Manor and walk towards Exhibition Square in front of the City Art Gallery. From Exhibition Square look at Bootham Bar. The arch dates from Norman times.

7. Bootham Bar to the Minster

Through Bootham Bar, walk along High Petergate until you arrive at the Minster.

The Anglo-Saxon Minster was badly damaged in the fighting with the Normans. When William the Conqueror took York he appointed Thomas of Bayeaux as his new Archbishop. He patched up the church only to see it be devastated again in 1075 when the Vikings invaded for the last time. Rather than repairing the Saxon church once more, Archbishop Thomas decided to use what once had been the Roman principia of the fortress as the site of a new cathedral. Re-using much of the fallen Roman masonry, he built a cathedral 110 metres long with walls that were 2.1 metres thick. Once it was complete, it was faced with painted white plaster, adorned with red lines for decoration. The huge white building would have towered over all the other buildings in the city, visible for miles around, testament to the power of William, the Norman king. It had taken only twenty years to build. In 1291, Archbishop Walter Grey began work on the new Gothic Minster that stands in front you today, which took 250 years to complete. Some of the remains of the original Norman Minster can be seen in the Undercroft Museum of the Minster.

Optional Visit: York Minster www.yorkminster.org

8. The Minster to The Norman House, Stonegate

Leave the Minster Yard and the statue of Constantine via the little street to the right called Minster Yard. Cross Petergate and enter Stonegate. Walk along Stonegate until you reach the passageway on the right between 52 and 54 Stonegate.

In 1939 two houses were demolished on Stonegate to reveal York's oldest house, dating from the 12th century. Its survival is due to the fact that it was built from stone, not timber. You are standing in what would have been the inside of the house, looking at two magnesian limestone walls. The undercroft, one metre below where you are standing, would have been used for storage and the first-floor hall would have been lit by windows. You can see one of these windows, relatively intact today. Glass would have been a luxury, so the windows only had shutters. In the 12th and 13th centuries Jewish financiers helped to create an economic boom in York and as Jewish owners may have had the necessary wealth, it is suggested that the house once belonged to someone of the Jewish community. The need for security from possible anti-Semitic attacks could explain why the house was built of stone. The surviving window is very similar to a house in Lincoln where Aaron the Jew was known to have lived, suggesting that both were constructed at the same time.

9. Norman House to Davygate

Return to Stonegate and turn right. Walk to the end of the street and at St Helen's church, turn left. On Davygate look for the plaque that describes Davy Hall.

Davy Hall once stood on the corner of Davygate and New Street, built onto the old wall of the Roman fortress. It was the home of the Lardiner of York, a role which began in the 1180s. After the Conquest, the new rulers established some harsh laws in York. Not only was it a crime to hunt in the huge Forest of Galtres, which lay to the north, the Normans also wanted to ensure that there would always be a plentiful supply of food available, just in case the King decided to visit York. To this end the role of Lardiner was created. The first Lardiner of York was David, who probably gave his name to the hall. The location of the hall gave him quick access to the market in St Sampson's Square where he was entitled to take bread from the baker and ale from the brewer every Saturday, without paying for it. In 1168 the Lardiner's powers were challenged in a legal battle, but to no avail. It wasn't until the Lord Mayor of York sued in 1253 that the right to take provision from the market was ended. However, Davy Hall was still used as a prison for poachers. The town council could do nothing about it as the hall was the property of the Crown. By 1427 Davy Hall lay in ruins and in the 17th century it was converted into tenement houses.

10. Davygate to St Cuthbert's, Peaseholme Green

From Davygate walk past Betty's Tearoom and proceed to St Sampson's Square. Continue walking as the street becomes Parliament Street. At the end of Parliament Street turn left onto Pavement. Walk past Lady Peckett's Yard and Herbert's House and follow the road (Stonebow) until it becomes Peaseholme Green. On the left you will find St Cuthbert's church.

St Cuthbert's is the oldest church in York after the Minster, dating from Norman times. The east wall of the chancel is built from Roman masonry from the fortress. It was the Normans who began the widespread pillaging and re-use of Roman masonry. The original building was restored and rebuilt in 1417 by William de Bowes, Lord Mayor of York. It is now St Cuthbert's House of Prayer.

11. St Cuthbert's Peaseholme Green to the Red Tower, Foss Islands Road

After leaving the church, turn left and walk to the traffic lights on the busy main road. Turn right onto Foss Islands Road. Walk for approximately 400 metres until you arrive at the Red Tower on the right-hand side of the road.

In 1068 William the Conqueror decided to damn the River Foss to flood the moat around York Castle. This caused the river to flood the area where you are standing now. It became known as the King's Fishpool, giving the king a plentiful supply of fish. The Red Tower was constructed here as a look-out post. However, the original tower was not red nor made of bricks. Little is known about the original, but it was probably squat and square. This tower was constructed in the 1480s after Richard III discussed repairing the walls with the city council. Bricks were used because they were cheaper than stone. Because York was naturally defended by the River Foss, the Normans did not feel the need to build any city walls, which is why today there are no walls where you are standing. You have now completed your walk. Well done.

York Walls Walk

In AD 71 the Romans dug earthwork ramparts and topped them with wooden palisades to create their fortress in what is now the northern corner of York. You will walk on a section of the modern wall that still follows the line of the Roman wall today. The Vikings extended the northern Roman ramparts and the Normans built two gateways, a tower and put up the walls beside St Mary's Abbey to protect the monks. However, the Normans decided not to extend the walls along what is now Foss Islands Road, believing that the River Foss was a natural defence. Therefore, at this point, you will need to leave the walls to later rejoin them beyond the river. Although the walls are the most complete of any city in Europe, they are not a full circuit and you will need to descend and walk on pavements to rejoin later. After 1319 it was decided to strengthen the city walls due to repeated attacks by the Scots. Consequently, the remaining sections of wooden walls were rebuilt in stone and barbicans were added to the front of the bars (gateways). By Georgian times some citizens began to view the walls as romantic ruins and slowly incorporated parts of them into their gardens, particularly along the section beside the Minster. Meanwhile to the Lord Mayor and the City Corporation the walls were becoming an annoyance because made it difficult for carts and carriages to move around. Furthermore, they were expensive to repair. Around 1800 the City Corporation knocked down a small section of the south wall. The Archbishop of York took action, suing the council, demanding that to be paid damages because he could no longer collect the tolls from people going through a gate to a fair which he had the right to hold. Although the Corporation petitioned Parliament to gain the right to demolish the walls, it was unsuccessful and a campaign began not only to save the walls, but to create a public path along them. York artist William Etty (1787-1849) was an influential member of this campaign. However, by the 1830s the Corporation was still knocking down bits of walls, whilst repairing and embellishing other sections. By the 1880s the city leaders had repaired and restored almost all of them. Nevertheless, they were faced with a new problem. Many people on the northern section who had incorporated the walls into their gardens did not want walkers staring down into what they considered their private space. Edwin Gray, the son of the Mayor and owner of what is now Gray's Court Hotel, said he would sue the corporation for trespass if they tried to touch "his" walls. A deal was reached by 1887 and the walls were given back to the city and a public footpath established along them, of approximately 3.5 miles. Look out for the plaque to Edwin Gray near Gray's Court. It states that he "restored" the walls to the city. Perhaps the plaque was part of the deal! So, as you enjoy your walk along the city walls, remember the famous saying about the city. "York: where the streets are gates, the gates are bars and the bars are pubs". In reality there are four main bars (fortified gateways), two smaller gateways with more modern stonework and one postern (a very small gateway defended by a tower), as well as frequent interval towers. There are also great views of some of the many important buildings of the city, such as the Minster.

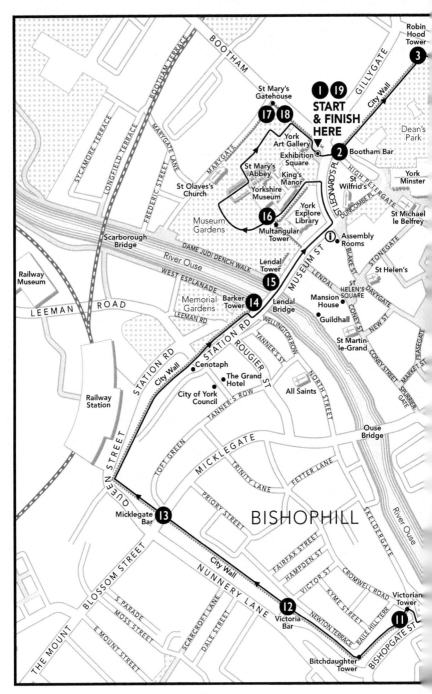

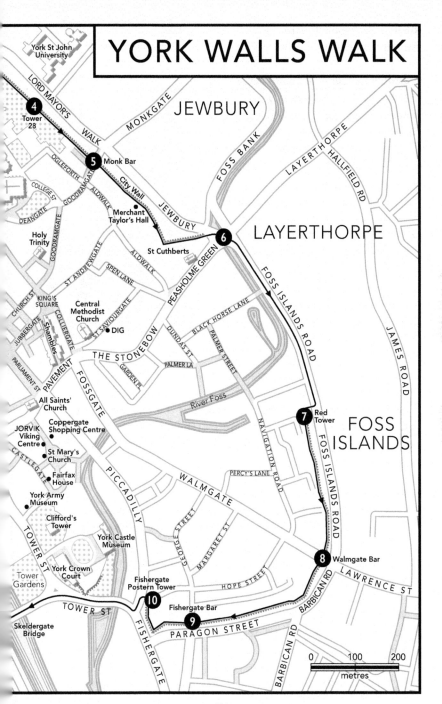

YORK WALLS WALK

York St John University

Tower 28 ④

LORD MAYOR'S WALK

⑤ Monk Bar

MONKGATE

JEWBURY

OGLEFORTH

COLLEGE ST

GOODRAMGATE

ALDWALK

City Wall

JEWBURY

FOSS BANK

LAYERTHORPE

HALLFIELD RD

DEANGATE

Holy Trinity

Merchant Taylor's Hall

St Cuthberts

⑥

LAYERTHORPE

GOODRAMGATE

ST ANDREWGATE

SPEN LANE

ALDWALK

PEASHOLME GREEN

CHURCH ST

KING'S SQUARE

JUBBERGATE

Central Methodist Church

ST SAVIOURGATE

DIG

THE STONEBOW

DUNDAS ST

BLACK HORSE LANE

PALMER STREET

FOSS ISLANDS ROAD

JAMES ROAD

Shambles

COLLIERGATE

GARDEN PL

PALMER LA

PARLIAMENT ST

PAVEMENT

FOSSGATE

River Foss

All Saints' Church

JORVIK Viking Centre

Coppergate Shopping Centre

⑦ Red Tower

FOSS ISLANDS

St Mary's Church

Fairfax House

PICCADILLY

WALMGATE

NAVIGATION ROAD

PERCY'S LANE

FOSS ISLANDS ROAD

York Army Museum

CASTLEGATE

Clifford's Tower

York Castle Museum

GEORGE STREET

MARGARET ST

TOWER ST

York Crown Court

⑧ Walmgate Bar

LAWRENCE ST

Tower Gardens

TOWER ST

Fishergate Postern Tower

⑩

HOPE STREET

BARBICAN RD

BARBICAN RD

Skeldergate Bridge

FISHERGATE

Fishergate Bar

⑨

PARAGON STREET

BARBICAN RD

0   100   200
metres

51

Start: Exhibition Square
Finish: Exhibition Square

1. Exhibition Square to Bootham Bar

Stand in Exhibition Square by the statue of the artist William Etty and admire Bootham Bar. Etty, famous for his nudes, was an important member of the campaign to save the city walls. The original Roman gateway lies beneath the bar. The front of the bar was rebuilt in 1719 and again in 1832. Its barbican was demolished in 1832. The little figures on the parapet have replaced the original ones, as have the painted stone shields on the front of the bar. The highest is the royal coat of arms. Below are two coats of arms of York (the red cross of St George emblazoned with red lions). The three statues that surmount the bar

show a medieval lord mayor, a knight and a mason. They were created by a Victorian stonemason whose workshop was next to the bar.

Go up the Victorian steps to the right of the bar and you will find yourself in the room above the bar's archway. Leave the room by the opposite doorway to which you entered and walk along the northern section of the walls.

2. Bootham Bar to Robin Hood Tower

You are about to walk over the whole north corner of the Roman legionary fort of Eboracum. As you proceed the walls will overlook Dean's Court, the garden of the Minster. The Dean is in charge of the Minster and its grounds. Within the garden is the Minster Library, which was once the palace of the Archbishop of York before he moved to Bishopthorpe. All the lovely houses along this section are connected to the administration of the Minster.

When you arrive at the angle in the corner of the walls, you will have arrived at Robin Hood Tower.

Robin Hood Tower is a Victorian replacement for a ruined medieval tower variously known as Bawling Tower (1370), Frost Tower (1485) and Robin Hood Tower (1622). It is circular with eight cruciform arrow slits.

3. Robin Hood Tower to Tower 28

Further along you will find Tower 28 with two turrets, which was built by the Victorians. About 70 metres further on there are steps that lead down to Grays Court. Archaeologists believe that the Porta Decumana of the Roman fortress lies just inside the grounds. The oldest part of this Grade 1 listed building dates back to 1080 and was commissioned by the first Norman Archbishop of York to provide the official residence for the treasurers of York Minster. It is now a privately owned hotel with a pleasant café.

4. Tower 28 to Monk Bar

At the end of this section of the walls you will arrive at Monk Bar. This is the tallest and strongest of the bars. Go down the steps and explore the bar from ground level. Watch out for traffic.

On the **interior** city side of the bar the wall and windows are the original medieval ones and as these were not defensive, they are larger than the windows on the exterior. This is the only bar to have its portcullis complete with the mechanism in working order. The gatehouse was built a century after the bar and now houses the Richard III Experience Museum. It is free to enter the gift shop where you can see the mechanism and the garderobe (toilet). Inside the bar itself you will see a blocked doorway. This is from the time that traders were stopped and made to pay "murage", a tax to enter the city. Under the arch you will see the spikes of the portcullis. Further in you can see the "murder holes" through which objects were dropped in an attack. On the exterior wall of the bar you will see arrow slits and two small square holes which were for cannon to fire out of. The small, metal studded wooden doors at each side of the bar are where the barbican, which was demolished in the 19th century used to be. The barbican, removed in 1825, would have stretched out to where you are standing. If an attacker got through, they would find themselves in the "killing ground" - trapped by the portcullis and surrounded by defenders.

Optional Visit: Richard III Experience www. richard111experience.com

Go up the steps on the other side of the bar and continue along the walls.

Very soon you will see the brick dome of a Georgian icehouse cut into the ramparts below. Notice the large medieval building partly cut into the ramparts ahead of you. This is the Merchant Taylor's Hall, dating from the fourteenth century, is the ancient guild hall of the tailors, drapers and hosiers.

As you walk between Monk Bar to Layerthorpe you will pass above a supermarket and a car park. This area of York is called Jewbury. (Look for the star of David set into the paving). The supermarket and car park are built on what was formerly the Jewish Quarter of the city.

Jewish people have lived in York since the twelfth century and were invited here to help finance economic development. In 1190, the local population's resentment over their debts to the Jewish financiers forced approximately 150 men, women and children of the Jewish community to take refuge in what is now Clifford's Tower. Rather than being killed by the baying mob the outside, tragically they committed mass suicide in the tower, killing each other, then setting fire to the tower. Despite this horrific incident, by the mid 1200s, over 200 Jewish people still lived in the city, until all Jewish people were expelled from the country in 1290 by Edward 1. Before the supermarket and car park were built an archaeological dig took place and a cemetery with approximately 500 graves was discovered. It was found that the first burials were made in 1230. In 1984 the skeletons were returned to Jewbury for a reburial supervised by the Chief Rabbi, 700 years after they were first interred. The site of the cemetery is now the car park where a plaque commemorates this event.

At this point you will need to leave the city walls and carefully cross the road to proceed by the side of the River Foss, which was used by the Normans as a natural defence of the city. Follow the main road, Foss Islands Road, by the side of the river and beyond until you arrive at the Red Tower on your right.

Years ago the Foss was a large, marshy lake that attackers could not easily cross. In around 1068 William the Conqueror ordered that the river be damned to create a moat around his castle and a lake called The King's Fishpool. Over the years it was a struggle to keep this area clean. In 1330 Edward III ordered that the area be cleaned up, complaining that there was an "abominable smell abounding in the city more than any other realm from the dung and manure and other filth and dirt wherewith the streets and lanes are filled and obstructed." In 1407 you could be fined 100 shillings for "throwing filth into the Foss to the prejudice of the royal fishery." Later the ordinary people who lived in this deprived area complained that they could not hear the priest in their parish church because of the barking of the dogs which were fighting over the butchers' waste dumped outside. By 1832 the area had become a health hazard and a suspected cause of the cholera epidemic. Ironically, the Corporation's solution was to financially incentivise people to dump their rubbish in the King's Fishpool to raise the ground level. Then in 1899 they built the Italianate tower chimney (now in the supermarket car park opposite) to burn the city's rubbish. Nicknamed "the destructor", the heat from the incinerator was used to generate electricity. Now defunct, this area of York is still used to manage rubbish today, with the city's waste recycling centre nearby.

The Red Tower was commissioned by Richard III (1452-1485) to replace an earlier Norman one. Built as a watchtower as part of a series of measures to strengthen the defences to the east of the city, bricks were cheaper than stone and there was a brickworks nearby. However, the decision to use bricks angered local stonemasons because they were not being employed to build the tower. Several of them began to harass the bricklayers and even stole their tools. Unfortunately, in 1491, one of the bricklayers was murdered by a pair of stonemasons. Christopher Horner and William Hindley (who created the statues of the Kings of England in York Minster) were charged with the murder and later acquitted.

7. The Red Tower to Walmgate Bar

Go behind the Red Tower to pick up the wall-walk once more.

As you walk along the ramparts look out for musket loops and cross-shaped arrow slits. Four hundred years after it was built the wall-walk here seems to have been one of the bits used as a recreational footpath long before the Victorians did their restorations and established the present paved wall walk. Look for small brass markers embedded every 25metres along the middle of the wall to help those involved in maintenance to map problems that need attention. In Victorian times this area of the city was slum. After mounting pressure the Corporation bought the properties to demolish them. The properties that you see today are still owned by the council. This part of the city around the suburb of Walmgate grew up around 800 years ago and is the youngest part of the city.

8. Walmgate Bar

Descend the walls when you arrive at Walmgate Bar.

This is the only bar which still has its medieval barbican and still bears the scars of military attacks. From the interior of the bar you can go under the Elizabethan extension and past the 15th century oak doors. Look up and you will see the groove where the portcullis is. This bar suffered tremendously in the Siege of York (1644) during the English Civil War. From the exterior of the barbican you can see a hollow with radiating cracks, which is probably the result of being hit by a cannon ball. Smaller holes will have been caused by musket balls. Worst of all was a plan by the Parliamentarian army to enter the city by mining under the bar and blowing it up with gunpowder. Fortunately, the defenders of the walls captured an enemy soldier and during his interrogation found out about the plot. The clever defenders foiled the conspiracy by flooding the tunnel with water, so that it had to be abandoned. If you look at the bottom two courses of stone you can see cracks in them, a result of the undermining.

8. Walmgate Bar to Fishergate Bar

Now take the steps up to the ramparts on the other side of Walmgate Bar and continue along the walls to Fishergate Bar.

Fishergate Bar dates from around 1315. By 1440 it was rebuilt, becoming a major entry point into the city. A mere 50 years later it is thought to have burnt down, suggested by the reddened and cracked stones just before the archway. Look for the grooves that the portcullis would have slid in. From the exterior of the arch you will see a carving to commemorate the repairs of the walls that you have just walked along, completed at the expense of Lord Mayor William Todd in 1487. He was knighted for successfully repelling attacks on both Bootham and Fishergate bars by local people rebelling against a tax imposed by Henry VII. However, this bar was destroyed in the 1489 Peasant's Revolt and to save money on repairing it, the gateway was simply bricked up for 340 years. The tunnels on either side of the main gateway remind us that once other gateways would have been short tunnels through earth ramparts. See if you can find the arrow-shaped mason's mark in the tunnel next to the pub. The pub inside the walls to the right of the bar is called The Phoenix because it was burnt down in the fifteenth century trouble only to be reborn from the fire again like the mythical bird.

9. Fishergate Bar to Fishergate Postern Tower

Now take the steps up onto the walls on the side opposite the pub. Walk along until you arrive at Fishergate Postern Tower.

Built around 1505, once upon a time water would have lapped at the foundations of Fishergate Postern Tower, creating a natural defence for the city. Next to the tower is a small postern gate, which would have once been a discrete entrance to the city, useful in times of siege. The tower has four floors, a spiral staircase and several masons' marks. Can you find the garderobe chute where waste would have once dropped straight into the river? The battlements on the top of the tower were converted into a row of square windows in the 1500s. The Friends of York Walls lease the tower from the City of York Council. Entry is free on open days where you will find display information.

Optional Visit: www.yorkwalls.org.uk

10. Fishergate Postern Tower to Baile Hill

Carefully cross over two streets - Piccadilly and Clifford Street, then walk over Skeldergate Bridge.

There are no walls here because this is the section that was knocked down by the Victorians to the horror of the Archbishop of York who sued the Corporation.

Over the bridge on your right you will see a neat little Victorian tower with some steps leading up to it. At this point re-enter the wall walk.

As soon as you ascend the tower you will notice the motte of Baile Hill castle. In 1068 William the Conqueror built a second wooden castle here to control traffic on the River Ouse between this castle and York Castle by putting a chain across the river. Only the motte can be seen today as modern houses cover where the bailey would have been.

11. Baile Hill to Victoria Bar

Before you arrive at Victoria Bar you will pass the curiously named **Bitchdaughter Tower**. Fortunately, the name is likely to be a corruption of the French "biche doughter". By 1566 it was in poor condition and its stone was taken to repair York Bridge. It was then probably rebuilt in 1645.

12. Victoria Bar

Victoria Bar was built to honour the new Queen. When it was cut through the walls, it was discovered that a medieval gate had been here. Records of the walls show that there was once a gate called Lounelith or "Lonely Gate" and this is perhaps the site of it. It is probable that the section of wall that you have just walked upon was made from the remains of Roman stone found in the colonia (civilian town) that grew up across the river from the legionary fort. You may wish to descend and read the information board on the ground floor of the bar.

13. Victoria Bar to Micklegate Bar

Continue along the walls until you arrive at Micklegate Bar.

Micklegate Bar is considered the principal gateway into the city because it guards the main road south to London. The lower section dates from the 12th century while the top storeys are from the 14th. Arriving monarchs would be greeted here while the heads of those whom they considered traitors would rot on spikes for years. Notice the stone figures on the top of the gateway. These probably replaced the spikes that displayed the putrefying heads. One of the most illustrious heads to have been spiked here was that of Richard II, Duke of York. In Shakespeare's play Queen Margaret orders, somewhat cleverly,

"Off with his head, and set it on York Gates,
So York may overlook the town of York."

From the city side of Micklegate Bar you will see two small, wooden doors. These used to lead to the wall walk around the defensive barbican, which was removed in 1826 because it was falling down. At the top of the façade is a royal coat of arms and below it the city's coat of arms with gold lions and a red cross. The lowest coat of arms is that of the Lord Mayor, responsible for an early restoration of the bar. The arch is thought to date from Norman times. The passage is built with some re-used Roman stone, including some sandstone coffins. When Henry VII (1457-1509) was victorious in the War of the Roses, he married Elizabeth of York in the Minster. You can find out about Henry VII in the little museum within the gatehouse of Micklegate Bar.

Optional Visit: Henry VII Experience www.richard111experience. org

14. Micklegate Bar to Barker Tower

Go up the steps on the other side of Micklegate Bar and continue your walk. On your left you will pass the current 1877 railway station. In 1841 George Hudson, Mayor of York and "Railway King", decided to build a station inside the city walls. To that end, controversially, he had four arches cut through the walls below you, two of them for trains to go through. Because trains had to reverse to continue on their route, it was decided to build a new station outside the walls.

As you continue along the walls, you will see to your left a small patch of green grass containing yew trees and some gravestones.

The old city moat was made into a graveyard in 1832 when there was a cholera epidemic so great that the city needed more space for graves. Dr John Stone, born in York in 1813, discovered the cause of cholera while living in London and is now considered the father of epidemiology.

Continuing, you will see a memorial below you to those who gave their lives in the two world wars. Behind this is the light-coloured headquarters of City of York Council and beyond is the 1906 Grand Hotel, which was once the main office of the North Eastern Railway.

15. Barker Tower to Lendal Tower

When the wall walk ends, carefully cross Rougier Street and find Barker Tower on your left.

Barker Tower was built opposite Lendal Tower, the larger tower on the opposite bank of the River Ouse so that a chain could be passed between the towers to control the river traffic.

Cross Ouse Bridge to arrive at Lendal Tower.

Lendal Tower has stood guard over the River Ouse since around 1300. In medieval times the great iron chain that was pulled from here across the river to Barker Tower controlled river traffic, charged tolls and protected the city in times of trouble. In 1677 the tower was leased for a term of 500 years to the York Waterworks Company. All running water was pumped from this tower into the pipes that ran through York. Notice the red brick building adjoining the tower. In 1836 it was decided to open an engine house dedicated to pumping the water. Since that time Lendal Tower has been used as offices, a store, a private residence and is now holiday accommodation.

16. Lendal Tower to Multangular Tower, Museum Gardens

Proceed into the city along Museum Street and enter The Yorkshire Museum Gardens. As you enter the garden, look to your right where you will see a wall with a tower on the corner.

This section of wall dates from the time that the Romans decided to rebuild their wooden ramparts in stone. The 6th Legion Victrix replaced the 9th Legion Hispana in the third century AD and was probably ordered by Septimius Severus to carry out the work. Notice the fine lines of terracotta bricks in the masonry. It is believed that the Multangular Tower is later than the wall and may have been ordered by Constantine the Great.

17. Multangular Tower

Walk up the little path among the rockery to the left of the Multangular Tower and explore it from behind.

Notice along the side of the library there are two sets of walls. The nearest are the original Roman walls and the furthest are the medieval walls. At the end of this section of wall you will find the Anglian Tower, so named because it was constructed by the Anglo-Saxons.

18. Multangular Tower - St Mary's Gatehouse

Leave the tower and walls by the same path on which you arrived. Back in the gardens of the museum, walk beyond the colonnaded museum and then turn right, following the path beside the ruins of St Mary's Abbey. Leave the museum gardens by the gate into the Edible Wood.

As you walk through the garden into the sculpture park behind York City Art Gallery, you will be able to admire the walls of St Mary's Abbey and in the corner, St Mary's Gatehouse. The original walls date from the 1260s. In 1318 the abbot gained permission to raise the height of the wall and crenellate it, possibly to protect the abbey from disgruntled local people who repeatedly rebelled against unpopular taxes levied on them for placing their market stalls (booths) outside Bootham Bar. The gatehouse and its lodge formed part of a range of buildings that linked to the church of St Olave. Work on the gatehouse was underway in 1314 and 1320, although the surviving structures are mostly of 15th century origin.

19. York City Art Gallery Sculpture Garden - Exhibition Square

Walk down the side of the back of the art gallery and you will emerge into Exhibition Square where your walk started.

Notice to your left that you are protected by the last remaining section of the city walls and that you have returned to your starting point. Well done. You have completed your walk!

Medieval Walk

York's medieval city was built over a Roman one. In the Middle Ages York reached its zenith of beauty and importance. The narrow streets with projecting dwelling-houses, inn and shops were crowded with busy and prosperous people. Ships loaded and unloaded their cargoes up and down the River Ouse. The city walls were rebuilt and strengthened. Monks and priests looked after the people spiritually and physically and the Minster gradually grew from the work of the throngs of stonemasons, glaziers and carpenters. During this walk you will learn of the importance of the guilds in York's history. While there were several friaries and priories in medieval York, the Dissolution of the Monasteries has left little trace of them. Nevertheless, the remains of the Bedern precinct hint at the privilege of those associated with the church in those times.

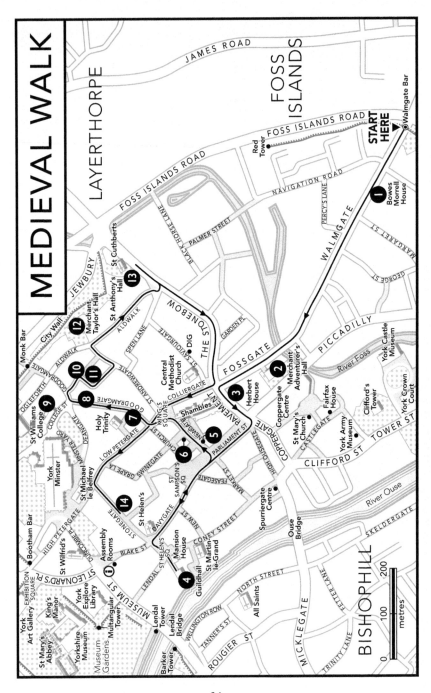

MEDIEVAL WALK

1. Bowes Morrell House, Walmgate

From Walmgate Bar, walk into the city where you will find Bowes Morrell House on the left.

In 1396 a licence was granted for the building of four houses in the churchyard of St Peter's. This building is believed to be the only remaining one of the four, as the dimensions of Bowes Morrell House match those stipulated in the licence. Perhaps it functioned as the vicarage of St Peter's. It is a timber-framed house with an open hall with no known parallel in York. The building was restored in 1966 by York Conservation Trust which named it after one of its co-founders, Dr John Bowes Morrell.

2. The Merchant Adventurer's Hall, Fossgate

Walk from Walmgate until it becomes Fossgate. On the left you will find the ornate archway of the Merchant Adventurer's Hall.

The company of the Merchant Adventurers came together in 1357 to form a guild and to build the hall. Predominantly textile merchants by trade, in 1581 they were granted a licence by Elizabeth 1 that allowed them to control commerce in the city. To become an entrepreneur in York you had to be a Freeman of the Company of the Merchant Adventurers. If you were not the daughter or widow of a Freeman, then as a woman you were not allowed to trade. There have been many additions and changes to the Hall over the years, but the main functions of business and charity remain the same today. The chapel in the Undercroft was once a hospital and is one of the oldest timber-framed buildings in York.

Optional Visit: www.merchantadventurershall.org

3. Herbert House, Pavement

Leave the hall via the gate onto Piccadilly. Turn right and walk to the end of the street.

At the corner turn right to find the timber-framed Herbert House.

The property dates from 1557 when a deed recorded the purchase of the house from the Merchant Adventurers' Company by Christopher Herbert and his wife in Elizabeth for the sum of approximately £54. Herbert became Lord Mayor of York in 1573, as well as Governor the Merchant Adventurers for the following two years. Sir Thomas Herbert was born in the house in 1606 and was a true seventeenth century cavalier, traveller and adventurer, going on a mission to the Shah of Persia. In 1647 Thomas Herbert supported Charles 1 and for the next two years was a constant personal attendant on the king. Though he remained in London until after the restoration of Charles II, he escaped the onset of the plague there and spent his last years in York where he bought 9 High Petergate and he wrote his memoirs.

4. The Guildhall, St Helen's Square

Walk up Parliament Street, the wide street flanked by shops. Walk beyond St Sampson's Square and along Davygate until you arrive at St Helen's Square. Turn left and find the pink and white Mansion House. To the right of the Mansion House is a passageway. Go down this passageway to find the Guildhall.

Although the Merchant Adventurers was a very powerful guild, the Guildhall is important as it was built to house council meetings. It was first recorded as the Common Hall in 1378. In 1445, the City Corporation and St Christopher's Guild agreed to share the expenses of building a new hall with a chamber at the west end, a cellar at the east, and other buildings including pantry and buttery. The first council meeting was held here in 1459. In 1646 a room was used by the Parliamentarian Roundheads to pay out £200,000 to the Scots for the surrender of Charles 1. A stained-glass window is first known to have been inserted about 1680. In the 1942 during the Baedeker raids by the German Luftwaffe, which targeted cultural and historic sites, a bomb fell on the roof of the Guildhall and caused a massive fire. The stone shell of the building was restored, and the Guildhall reopened by Queen Elizabeth, the Queen Mother in June 1960.

5. 4 Jubbergate

Return to Parliament Street and take the short street called Jubbergate, beyond St Sampson's Square and Goodramgate, into the Shambles Market area.

Find the free-standing, timber-framed building in and amongst the market stalls. When it was originally built in 1600, it would have adjoined other properties before they were destroyed. It is of two-storeys with gables. Photographs from the 19th and 20th centuries show that the timbering was plastered over, and the approach to it was cobbled. Jubbergate first appears around 1200 as Bretgate and by 1280 was called 'Joubrettegat – 'the street of the British in the Jewish quarter', showing that there was an important Jewish community in the city in the early medieval period.

6. 12 Newgate

Turn left onto Newgate and then turn right to find number 12.

This is probably the second oldest house in York. The range from number 12 to number 15 Newgate represents the surviving units of a row of timber-framed houses built in the churchyard of St. Sampson in 1337. Sir Hugh Botner, chaplain of York, was granted a licence to build houses on part of the cemetery along the street called Le Newgate. The rent from the buildings would help to fund the church. No. 12 represents one original tenement, of which there were originally ten or twelve, each self-contained with one room upstairs and one down. The upper room would be open to the roof. No. 12 was heightened in the early nineteenth century to create an attic and all the windows are modern.

7. Our Lady's Row, Goodramgate

Leave the Shambles Market area by walking across the top of the Shambles and into King's Square. Cross the square and turn right onto Goodramgate. On the left you will find Our Lady's Row.

(c) Peter K Burian

Dating from 1316 this is the earliest row of houses surviving in the city. Behind the row lies Holy Trinity Church, almost hidden from view. The houses were built in the original churchyard to provide rental income towards the church's running expenses. The houses are very simple, made of plastered timber framing with roofs of curved tiles (pantiles). When it was built the row had two storeys and eleven bays. Generally, each bay formed a single home with one room on each floor. The basic structure of seven of the bays remains largely intact today. In 1827 the survival of the row was threatened when it was proposed to expose the church to the street once more. Fortunately, the threat was averted and the row survived.

8. 43 Goodramgate

Now walk along Goodramgate to find the following medieval buildings.

a) 43 Goodramgate

In the late 15th or early 16th century this timber-framed building would have run some considerable distance back from the street. It was altered in the 19th century by having the jetties cut back and the front re-faced in brick. The back wall was removed, the original floors were taken out and the floor levels were altered. The frontage is in mottled brick. It was restored at the instigation of Cuthbert Morrell, the brother of John Bowes Morrell, in around 1932 and transferred to the ownership of York Conservation Trust in 1957.

b) 45 Goodramgate

Like number 43 this large timber-framed building would once have run some considerable distance back from the street front and was built in the late 15th or early 16th century to a height of three storeys. The upper floors are jettied at the front, but not the rear. This property was also restored at the instigation of Cuthbert Morrell in around 1932 and transferred to the ownership of this Trust in 1957.

c) 49 and 51 Goodramgate, Wealden Hall

Purchased in 1931 by Cuthbert Morrell at the same time as number 49, this property was originally of four timber box framed bays. The roof was constructed to form a hall. Dating from the late 15th or early 16th century, it is a Wealden type of hall, which is very rare in the north of England with only twenty to be found outside Kent and the Home Counties. It is safe to say that this property was originally for a higher status occupant, as it would have cost a considerable amount to build.

9. St William's College

Continue along Goodramgate until it is intersected by College Street where you will find St William's College.

This was once the house of a canon of the Minster, but due to the rowdy behaviour of the chantry priests of York Minster, they were moved here from Bedern Precinct in 1465. Chantry priests were paid by patrons to sing for their souls and the Minster wanted to keep a closer eye on them. At the time of the Dissolution of the Monasteries (1536-41), there were 28 priests and one provost living here. Just before the Civil War of 1644, Charles 1 set up a printing press here to distribute propaganda in his favour. The building has been altered many times over the years with the frontispiece dating from the middle of the 17th century. Look for the carving of St William flanked by armorial shields above the entrance. It was substantially restored 1902 by Temple Moore. It is of 2 storeys with 10 bays and there is an interior courtyard.

10. Bedern Chapel

Walk back to Goodramgate and find Bedern archway on the left. Walk through the arch to find Bedern Chapel on the right.

The word bedern is derived from Old English bede meaning prayer and ærn meaning house. This was the chapel of the aforementioned chantry priests or Vicars Choral. They maintained a daily pattern of prayer and were the deputies of the senior canons. In 1252 the Bedern Vicars were the first in England to be formed as a college with their very own precinct with three buildings in this area. After beginning as choir boys, new vicars were inducted in Bedern Chapel with the last induction here in 1919.

11. Bedern Hall

Continue beyond Bedern Chapel to Bartle Garth. Turn right to find Bedern Hall.

The Bedern Vicars formed a strong community, dining together in this hall once a day at around 5pm. Archaeological evidence suggests that they lived well with a high-status diet, including venison, and they possessed some prestigious glassware. Despite their religious duties they did get themselves into trouble over the years including brawling, riotous drinking, carrying swords and promiscuity. Although having a regular mistress seems to have figured quite low on their list of transgressions. At the height of their prosperity in the 1380s the Bedern Vicars had an established hierarchy for their own management and possessed extensive estates. However, in

1547 paid masses for the dead were banned so their most significant source of income disappeared. In 1548 the priests were allowed to marry, which destabilised their collegiate life. In 1574, their communal dining ceased. In 1868 the remaining vicars ceded their rights in Bedern to the church, although the vicars continued to own the chapel. Later Bedern declined into a slum in the 1800s. In the 1980s the hall of the Vicars Choral was painstakingly reconstructed.

12. Merchant Taylor's Hall

With your back to the hall turn right on Bartle Garth. Then turn right onto Bedern. Turn left onto St Andrewgate. Then turn left onto Aldwark where you will find the Merchant Taylor's Hall.

The earliest reference to the guild dates back to 1387, while the hall dates from 1415. In medieval days the tailors were closely associated with the religious and charitable fraternity of St. John the Baptist, which built the present hall. During this period they enjoyed a golden age, playing a major role in the social as well as economic life of the city. From the 17th century boys from the city and nearby villages were apprenticed. Until the 1830s the Merchant Taylors' Company, which included a few women among its members, was essentially a working body of master tailors, York freemen of some substance but rarely of outstanding status or wealth. Only by leasing their hall for either educational, theatrical or social purposes did they succeed in preserving the building into the early nineteenth century.

13. St Anthony's Hall

Walk down Aldwark away from the city centre until you arrive at Peaseholme Green. Turn left and find St Anthony's Hall on the left.

This is the fourth and last of the surviving York guild halls, with a chequered history and many uses. First of all King Henry VI granted a charter in 1446 for the founding of the guild of St Martin. Because the hall and a chapel were then built on the site of the chapel for St Anthony, the hall took this name. By 1453 it had a hospital chapel that was used by patients and members of the guild. By 1569 St Anthony's was being used as a workhouse for the poor, where weaving was among the main chores of the work force. In 1586 part of the hall had been converted into a house of correction and a place of detention and work for minor criminals. In the early 17th century the hall was used as a knitting school for poor children. However, by 1655 the lower part of the hall was back in use as a house of correction and this continued until 1814. During the English Civil War (1625 – 1649) the hall was also used as an ammunition storeroom, military hospital and a prison. In 1705 the Blue Coat charity used the main hall for teaching, while using the aisles for sleeping and eating. The ground floor houses kitchens and service rooms. The Blue Coat charity occupied St Anthony's hall up until 1946. In 1953 York Civic Trust came into management of St Anthony's guildhall.

14. Mulberry Hall, Stonegate

With your back to the hall, turn right and walk back towards the centre of the city. At Colliergate turn right and walk up beyond King's Square and onto Low Petergate. Continue until you arrive at Stonegate on the left. Find Mulberry Hall, numbers 17 -19 on the left.

Dating from the fifteenth century a wing was added in the late sixteenth century and it was restored in the twentieth century. This timber-framed building was most likely the house of a rich merchant. It has many interesting architectural features such as the first and second floor oriel windows with square and diamond leaded lights. Well done. You have completed your walk.

Snickelways Walk

The term "snickelway" was coined by local author Mark W. Jones in 1983 in his best-selling book "A Walk around the Snickelways of York". The word is an amalgamation of "snicket", "ginnel" and "alleyway", each of which mean "passageway". In contrast to the rigid street layout that the Romans left behind, snickelways thread and wind in delightfully mysterious ways, making discovering them great fun as you emerge from dark, narrow and twisting tunnels onto bustling thoroughfares, forcing you to see York from a completely new perspective. It is probably the Vikings who bestowed the city with many of the cut-throughs, which were later added to in medieval times. The often-quirky names give a flavour of York's eclectic past. It is claimed that there are approximately fifty snickelways in York today. This walk takes in those which cluster secretively around the centre of the city. You will need to do this walk before 5pm as some of the alleyways cut through historic properties which close for the evening.

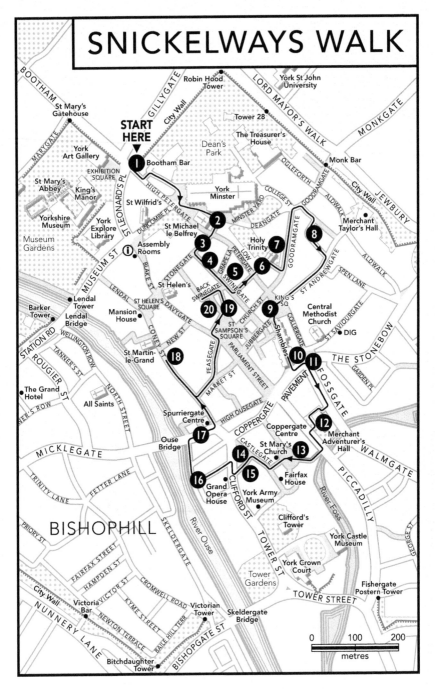

SNICKELWAYS WALK

Start: Bootham Bar
End: Back Swinegate

1. Bootham Bar

From Bootham Bar, enter the city and almost immediately on your left you will find the first snickelway - Little Peculiar Lane. Walk down Little Peculiar Lane until you emerge in Precentor's Court.

The precentor was in charge of the music at the Minster and here you will find many of the houses of those involved in the administration of York Minster.

2. Minster Yard to Minster Gates

To the right of the main entrance to the Minster you will find the statue of Constantine, the Great. Leave Minster Yard by the alleyway to the right called Minster Gates.

Notice the plaque on the wall on your left explaining the significance of the street. This street is closely associated with booksellers. Notice the statue of Minerva, goddess of learning, above the doorway on the building to the right.

3. Minster Gates to Stonegate

Minster Gates leads to Petergate. Cross Petergate and enter Stonegate. As you walk along Stonegate look out for the red devil, beside number 33 and the sign for Coffee Yard.

The red devil is here because in the 1880s printing was known as the "black art" due to the use of inks. The famous printer, Thomas Gent (1693-1778), had his workshop in this snickelway in the eighteenth century. Active for over fifty years, Gent was also an author. He worked from Coffee Yard using wood-block printing and his publications often focused on the history of York and its surrounding areas. York's first newspaper was printed here 1719.

Continue through the snickelway to find the stunning timber-framed building of Barley Hall, a reconstruction by York Archaeological Trust of what was once a hospice for Nostell Priory in West Yorkshire.

Optional Visits: www.barleyhall.co.uk

As you leave this snickelway, you will emerge onto Grape Lane.

4. Grape Lane to Swinegate

You are now in what would have once been the red light district of York. The name Grape Lane is a polite corruption of its much more sinister and illustrative name - Gropecunt Lane! It's hard not to feel pity for the poor women who had to earn their living from prostitution on what once have been this dark, dingy and dirty street.

5. Swinegate to Mad Alice Lane

Proceed straight ahead and walk along Swinegate. On your left you will find a snickelway. This is Lund's Court or formerly Mad Alice Lane.

Some people say that this snickelway takes its name from Alice Smith who lived here until 1825 and was hung for the crime of insanity. Some say she was hung for poisoning her husband. Others argue that there are no records of an execution of anyone called Alice Smith and she wouldn't have been hung for being insane anyway. Who knows? You will now emerge onto High Petergate.

6. Mad Alice Lane to Hornpot Lane

On High Petergate straight ahead, you will see another snickelway on the opposite side of the street. This is Hornpot Lane. Walk along it and you will emerge into the church yard of Holy Trinity.

Hornpot lane is so-called because a 14th century pit full of horns was found, proof that this was a trade at that time. After enjoying the serenity of the churchyard, leave by the arched gateway on the other side of the garden.

7. Holy Trinity to Goodramgate

Return to Goodramgate, turn left and walk to the junction at the end. Keep right on Goodramgate and look to your right where you will find a dark arched entrance. Enter to find Bedern Chapel lurking in the shadows.

This chapel once belonged to the Vicars-Choral of York Minster. They were a privileged group of men, also known as chantry priests, who were paid to sing for the souls of their dead patrons. This whole area was once a complex of buildings which served their needs, comprising of a chapel, a dining-hall and accommodation. By the 1840s this area was filled with slums where poverty and disease were rife, until it was finally cleared and a collection of warehouses and workshops grew up.

8 . Bedern Hall

Proceed beside Bedern Chapel to Bartle Garth. Turn right where you will find Bedern Hall.

Once the dining hall of the Vicars-Choral, it is now a wedding venue.

After exploring the hall, return to Bartle Garth to emerge onto St Andrewgate. Turn right on this street and walk along it until you arrive at King's Square.

9. King's Square to The Shambles

Look across the square and in the left corner you will see the top of one of the oldest streets in Britain - the Shambles.

At the top of the Shambles notice the information board that tells you that this street derives its name from "shamel" which refers to the benches that the butchers used to display their meat on. From 1190 onwards this street was home to up to 30 butchers at any one time and by 1830 there were still 25 left. As you walk down the street, notice several shops with meat hooks still above their windows. Look down at the channels on either side of the cobbles, used for the excess blood of the butchered animals to be washed away. Imagine the noise of terrified animals, corralled here, being driven down the street to their deaths. Imagine the unavoidable stench of blood in the air and the flies swarming around the hanging hanks of meat.

The Shambles has so many snickelways that Mark W. Jacobs described the walk along it as "the Great Shambles In-and Out" and the "Grand Slalom of the Snickelways". As you walk down you will arrive at number 35 on the right side, which is the shrine to Margaret Clitherow. Immediately before her shrine, turn right through a timbered arch. Suddenly you will find yourself in the Shambles Market. Keep walking down and you will find another snickelway on your left and suddenly you will be back on the Shambles. Rejoin the ancient street and then in a few metres along, find another snickelway which leads you straight back into the market. Continue in the same direction to find the final snickelway out of the market and lo and behold you are back on the Shambles again after having snaked your way along.

No wonder JK Rowling was inspired by this street to create Diagonalley!

Get ready for one last snickelway at the bottom of the street on the left. This is probably the most famous snickelway of York - Whip-Ma-Whop-Ma-Gate. **Enter Whip-Ma-Whop-Ma-Gate and proceed until you emerge opposite St Crux Church Hall.**

This street derives its name from "whitnourwhatnourgate" meaning "neither whit nor what street", suggesting that medieval York folk were somewhat scornful of this street.

10. Whip-Ma-Whop-Ma-Gate to Lady Peckett's Yard

Head towards the street that runs along the bottom of Whip-Ma-Whop-Ma-Gate (Pavement - probably so-called as it was the first street to be paved in York) and cross over to the fine timber-framed building called Herbert's House. To the right you will see the entrance to Lady Peckett's Yard.

11. Lady Peckett's Yard to Fossgate

Alice Peckett was the wife of John Peckett, Lord Mayor of York in 1701. Different names for this snickelway were first recorded in 1301 and 1312 and later it was known as Cheat's Lane. The house at the bottom is where the Pecketts lived and was built in the mid 16th century with alterations over subsequent centuries. It is now owned by York Conservation Trust.

12. Fossgate to Merchant Adventurer's Hall

After emerging onto Fossgate turn right and head along the street. After one hundred yards you will see on the right a small, impressive arched entrance with a gold coat of arms above it. This is the entrance to the Merchant Adventurer's Hall.

The Merchant Adventurers Hall was built in 1357 by textile merchants. It is the largest wood frame building in the world that is still used for its original purpose and well worth a visit.

Optional Visit: www.merchantshallyork.org

Leave the hall via the steps and gates on the opposite side to which you entered to emerge onto Piccadilly.

13. Piccadilly to Coppergate

From Piccadilly look across the road and you will see the entrance to a car park. Go through this modern snickelway to emerge into Coppergate.

You are now in the heart of what was once the Viking nucleus of York, excavated between 1976 and 1981. Here you could make an optional visit to Yorvik Viking Centre to learn more about the finds in this part of York.

Optional Visit: www.yorvikvikingcentre.co.uk

14. Coppergate to Friargate

Leave Coppergate by walking up the side of St Mary's Church to emerge onto Castlegate. On Castlegate turn right and proceed along the street until you find Friargate on the left.

15. Friargate to Clifford Street

On Friargate you will find the Friends Meeting House of the Quakers, dating from the nineteenth century.

Quakerism in York dates back to around the 1640s. The founder of the Quaker movement, George Fox, visited York Minster in 1651. After making a point about God to the congregation he was literally thrown out of the building and down the steps. Fortunately, Quakerism is more tolerated today and has been hugely influential in the city due to many of the confectioners and chocolate manufacturers being of the Quaker faith. (See Chocolate Walk)

At the bottom of Friargate emerge onto Clifford Street.

16. Clifford Street to King's Staith

Carefully cross Clifford Street and walk towards the Grand Opera House. After the theatre turn right and head down Cumberland Street where you will emerge at the King's Staith and the River Ouse.

17. King's Staith to Bridge Street

Turn right and walk along the river past the pub on your right. Go up the steps and emerge onto Bridge Street. Turn right and go up Bridge Street until you see the Spurriergate Centre in front of you in what was once a church. Just before the Spurriergate Centre on the left you will see a small street called Church Street. Go up Church Street and explore what this hidden corner of York has to offer.

18. Church Street to Coney Street

On leaving Church Street you will emerge onto Spurriergate. Turn left and the street will become Coney Street. As you walk along Coney Street, notice that on the right there is a dark little alleyway up to the Judge's Court Hotel.

This Grade II listed townhouse was built in the early 18th century. Visiting judges attending the quarterly Assize Courts would stay here until 1806 when the grander Judges Lodging on Lendal became available. The house was then used as premises for law firms until it was converted into a hotel in 2013.

19. Coney Street to Finkle Street

Return to Coney Street and take the first right, walking up Market Street. When the street divides into two, take the left branch which now becomes Feasegate. At the end of Feasegate turn left onto Davygate. Then take an immediate right onto Finkle Street.

Once upon a time Finkle Street had the dubious nickname of "Murky Peg Lane" and "Mucky Peg Lane". With its proximity to Grape Lane, it's not hard to realise that this area of York was once the place where desperate women would have sold themselves. Fortunately, the area has been cleaned up today!

20. Finkle Street to Back Swinegate

Walk up Finkle Street and look to the left to find your final snickelway - Nether Hornpot Lane. Walk along this snickelway until you arrive at Back Swinegate. You have now returned to the backstreets of York and have successfully completed your walk, hopefully without too much dizziness!

Georgian Walk

By the early 18th century, York was in economic decline. The River
Ouse had become silted up and consequently difficult to navigate,
while the city fathers had introduced a range of restrictive practices
that stifled free trade. Compounded by competition from burgeoning
industrial cities such as Hull and Leeds, York needed to try something
new to kick-start its economy. The city fathers took the decision
to turn York into the social capital of the North, a place where the
local gentry and aristocracy could come to spend the winter season.
The élite eagerly embraced the entertainments on offer in York as
this allowed them to avoid uncomfortable expeditions to London
on appalling roads, made all the more hazardous by frequent
encounters with highwaymen on journeys that could take several
days. Prolific architect John Carr (1723-1807) was employed to build
a truly grand grandstand at the Knavesmire racecourse and Lord

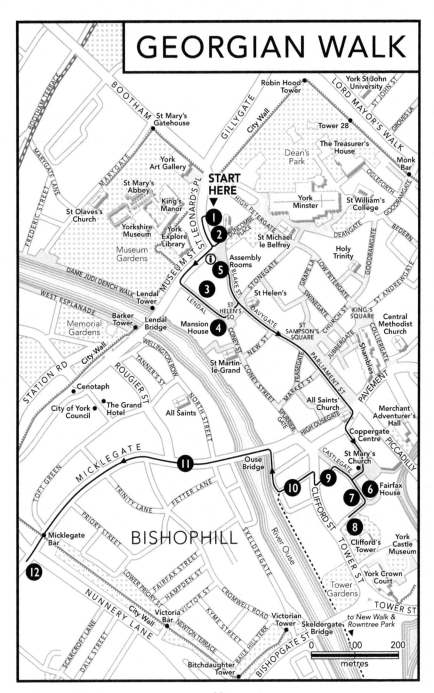

GEORGIAN WALK

Burlington (1694-1753) was called upon to design the Assembly Rooms, creating a social club fit for society's élite. The Assembly Rooms began a craze across the country for Palladian style buildings, that made York the height of fashion. To allow the glamorous Georgians to display themselves and take some exercise, in 1730 the New Walk along the River Ouse was created. By the 1750's York was packed with the great and the good who had purchased town houses, many of which are still visible along Micklegate today. After flirting, dancing, drinking, attending the races, the theatre or even an execution, they could then retire in style to their elegant residences. Georgian York owes a huge debt to the architect John Carr, who earned the sobriquet "Carr of York" due to his prolific contribution to the city's architecture. This walk takes in many of the Georgian buildings that the city is proud to offer, with ideas for optional extensions along the river at the end.

Start: York Theatre Royal, St Leonard's Place

End: Bar Convent, Blossom Street

1. York Theatre Royal, St Leonard's Place

Begin your walk outside York Theatre Royal.

The current façade dates from the 19th century and is neo-Gothic. However, the theatre in York was established in 1734 and some of the interior is from this period. Its most famous actor-manager was Tate Wilkinson (1739-1803) . For thirty-four years he staged plays to appeal to the gentry, engaging famous actresses such as Sarah Siddons and Dorothea Jordan, as well as bringing in novelty acts such as tightrope dancers, animals, bird imitators, tumblers, all with spectacular scenery and machinery.

2. Red House, Duncombe Place

Walk away from Exhibition Square towards York Tourist Information Office. At Duncombe Place turn left and you will now find yourself standing in front of Red House.

This Grade 2 listed town house was constructed in 1700 for Sir William Robinson, Lord Mayor of York. Dr John Burton (1709-1770) also lived here. Known as the "Man Midwife" for introducing the practice of delivering babies with women lying on their sides, rather than their backs, he also created a new type of forceps, known as "The Lobster Claw". He was part of a larger community of contemporary medics increasingly trying to professionalise the field of medicine.

3. The Judge's Lodging, Lendal

**From Red House cross
the street to the Tourist
Information Office in front of
you. Walk down Museum Street
beyond the public library and
take the first left on Lendal.
On the left you will see the
impressive Judge's Lodging, set
back from the street.**

The Judge's Lodging is a
Grade 1 listed building, erected
between 1711 and 1726. Originally built as a private residence for Clifton
Winteringham, a doctor who was appointed to York County Hospital in
1746. Winteringham made a ground-breaking study by collecting data over
twenty years to chart the rates of epidemics in the city, such as typhus.
The building took its present name in 1806 when it was bought by the
council for use as the residence of the judges who would visit York every
three months for the Assize Courts at York Castle, which dealt with the most
serious crimes.

4. The Mansion House

**Continue ahead along Lendal and after the alleyway on the right,
you will come across the pink and white façade of the Mansion
House facing into St Helen's Square.**

Completed in 1732 the Mansion House is the first purpose-built mayoral
home in the country. The architect is unknown, but likely to have been John
Etty. It holds one of the largest civic collections of silver in England, along
with a lot of mayoral regalia. Reputed to have been built to encourage the
Lord Mayor to spend more time in the city, it houses a portrait of George IV
that he donated on his visit here in the 18th century.

Optional Visit: Mansion House www.mansionhouseyork.com

5. The Assembly Rooms, Blake Street

Cross St Helen's Square towards Stonegate.

During the Georgian era St Helen's Square would have held the graveyard of St Helen's church. Crossing the graveyard made access to the new Assembly Rooms difficult, so it was moved and paved over.

Turn left onto Blake Street. Ahead you will see the impressive ionic columns of the Assembly Rooms.

Richard Boyle, third Earl of Burlington (Lord Lieutenant of Yorkshire 1725-32) was given carte blanche by the directors of the Assembly Rooms to design them in the manner that he thought proper. Influenced by the architecture that he had seen on his Grand Tour, in 1730 he aimed to reconstruct what the classical Roman architect Vitruvius described as an Egyptian Hall. Reputed to be the first Palladian style public building in the country, this was the place to see and be seen in Georgian times. Look inside the building and imagine the gentry dancing, drinking and socialising between the marbled Corinthian columns. On the right was the Round Room where gaming would take place. On the other side was the Refreshment Room where you could be served tea, coffee or chocolate. The exterior was designed later by Pritchett and Watson in 1828.

6. Fairfax House, Castlegate

Leave the Assembly Rooms and retrace your steps towards St Helen's Square. Keep straight ahead and walk along Davygate, pass St Sampson's Square and walk along Parliament Street to the traffic lights. Turn right here and then left into the Coppergate Centre. Leave the Coppergate Centre by St Mary's ch urch to emerge onto Castlegate. Turn left and you will find the impressive Fairfax House.

Fairfax House is the jewel in the crown of York's Georgian architecture. It was the winter townhouse of the 9th Viscount

Fairfax, Charles Gregory. After acquiring the property in 1759, Lord Fairfax employed Yorkshire architect John Carr to remodel it for him. At a cost of £10,000 he complained that the renovations that he had commissioned for his only surviving daughter, Anne, were taking all his money. Inside you can see why: gorgeous stucco work by Joseph Cortese and a fine Venetian window above the staircase, amongst other jems. Described by Simon Jenkins as "the finest townhouse in the country", it is well worth a visit to admire the amazing restoration carried out by York Civic Trust, as well as the tragic story of how the Viscount's family was devastated by smallpox. The house is furnished with the Noel Terry collection of furniture that he bequeathed to the Trust on his death. Outside the impressive indented entrance dates from the time that the house was used as dance hall. The less ostentatious doorway to the right would have been the original main entrance to the house and is flanked by two Tuscan columns holding up a pediment.

Optional Visit: Fairfax House www.fairfaxhouse.co.uk

7. Castlegate House

Opposite Fairfax House you will see another fine Georgian House set back from the road.

This is Castlegate House which was built for Peter Johnson, Recorder of York Minster, again by John Carr and finished in 1763. It has a porch with Tuscan columns and a pediment. Inside the staircase also has a Venetian window where there are other impressive features such as chimneypieces, doorcases and an Adam style ceiling. The house is currently a Masonic Lodge with entry limited to open days and special events.

8. Castle Complex

Leave Castlegate and walk towards Clifford's Tower. Find the green patch of land in the centre of the castle complex. This circular lawn is known as the "Eye of York".

Notice the entrance to the Castle Museum in front of you. This was once the **Debtor's Prison**, built between 1701 and 1705 in the English Baroque style. John Carr built the County Court to your right between 1773 and 1777. In 1780 he built **The Female Prison** on the left to reflect the Ionic façade of the County Court and to ease some of the overcrowding problems in the Debtor's Prison. As well as housing women, some men were imprisoned here, and it contained an infirmary and a chapel. Part of the Female Prison and all of the Debtor's Prison now house York Castle Museum, where you can experience what it would have been like to be a prisoner in Georgian times. Imagine the castle complex in the Georgian era. In 1727 Clifford's Tower was acquired by a private individual, Samuel Waud, who built a mansion in the grounds of this complex and turned the tower into a folly in his garden.

Optional Visit: York Castle Museum
www.yorkcastlemuseum.org.uk

9. Castlegate to Friargate

Return to Castlegate walking along it, away from Clifford's Tower.

Castlegate is so named because it leads to Clifford's Tower, also known as York Castle. The castle complex has always been the place of imprisonment in York. The condemned would be taken from the prison complex, along Castlegate to their place of execution. Dick Turpin would have been brought along this street to meet his end at the Knavesmire. Likewise, in 1746 the 22 men who had been condemned as traitors in the Jacobite Rebellion, after fighting in the Battle of Culloden, were forced along this street to their deaths on the Knavesmire.

10. Cumberland House

Find Friargate on the left of Castlegate. Walk down it to arrive at Clifford Street. Carefully cross Clifford Street and walk down Cumberland Street. Turn right to stand in front of Cumberland House.

Cumberland House was built around 1710 for William Cornwell, a tanner and brewer, who was Lord Mayor of York between 1712-3 and 1725-6. The façade overlooking the River Ouse has five bays and is in brick with stone dressings. Looking at the building from King's Staith, the basement would have been used for the storage of goods connected with Cornwell's trade. The house is thought to have acquired its name in honour of the Duke of Cumberland who may have resided here on 23 July 1746 on his journey from Scotland to London, following his victory at the Battle of Culloden on 16 April. Prince William, Duke of Cumberland, was the third and youngest son of King George II. His brutality at the Jacobite rebellion against his father earned him the nickname the "Butcher of Culloden".

11. Micklegate

At the end of King's Staith, go up the steps and onto Bridge Street. Turn left and follow the street until you arrive at Micklegate.

Although Micklegate was laid out by the Vikings and the name translates as "great street", it was the Georgians who took this street to its architectural zenith. Evidence suggests that it was a street for the upper class of York as far back as the 12th century. By the 18th century the street remained occupied by the aristocracy and merchants, with a few shops belonging to artisans. On race days the street would be bustling and teeming with the gentry arranging their carriages to transport them to the Knavesmire. Later in the 19th century many of the occupiers of the mansions began to move to suburban properties in Blossom Street and the Mount. At this time the number of shops and premises increased. Described by Pevsner as "the most rewarding street in York", some of the most interesting Georgian buildings on this street are as follows:

The Queen's Hotel: This was originally two early Georgian houses, each with a broad doorway. Inside a room dating from 1730 has panelling and Corinthian pilasters.

Numbers 35-37: The house dates back to the 17th century with an 18th century frontispiece.

Number 54: Notice the plaque for St Margaret's School for girls. This house is in fact Garforth House. Grade 1 listed due to the vast quantity of features of architectural interest both inside and outside, it dates from 1757 and was probably built by John Carr for Edmund and Elizabeth Garforth.

Number 88: Micklegate House was built for John Bourchier (1710-1759) whose ancestor Sir John Bourchier was one of the signatories of the warrant for the execution of King Charles 1. John Bourchier was a Lord Mayor of York and owned Beninbrough Hall to the north of York. Dated from 1752, this Grade 1 listed building has also been attributed to John Carr.

12. The Bar Convent, Blossom Street

Walk through Micklegate Bar to see The Bar Convent.

Like many Georgian buildings, the façade of 1786 fronts earlier buildings. The Chapel block was constructed between 1766- 1769. Work from this period was by Thomas Atkinson. There were later additions in the 18th century. Since its foundation The Institute of the Blessed Virgin Mary had always been vulnerable to religious intolerance and persecution and it is not a coincidence that the convent is located just outside the city walls, for its own protection. In 1696 the convent was attacked by an anti-Catholic mob. Keeping a low profile as a row of elegant Georgian townhouses, the spectacular domed chapel with fluted ionic columns is hidden from view, while a school is attached to the rear. The chapel is open to all those who wish to worship. There is a museum which charges an entry fee and a pleasant café where you could end your walk. Before you finish your walk, consider this: in 1746 Catholics were treated as second class citizens without equal rights to Anglicans. For seven years the nuns would have gone about their business next to Micklegate Bar while the heads of two of the 22 men executed for their part in the Catholic Jacobite Rebellion against George II would have gazed down on them. While the Georgian era was the age of splendour and elegance, at the same time brutal, Draconian punishments continued for those unfortunate enough to find themselves on the wrong side of the law. Well done. You have finished your tour of Georgian York.

New Walk Optional Extension: Return to King's Staith where you have visited Cumberland House. Walk along the bank of the River Ouse until you enter the section called New Walk. This was paved over in Georgian times in order to make York an attractive destination for the gentry. Imagine ladies in hooped skirts promenading along here with their parasols. There is a documented case of a lady being quite shocked one day when a man emerged from the river in the nude, after having had a bath in the water. Walk until you arrive at Millennium Bridge. Enter Joseph Rowntree Park. After exploring the park, you can return to the bank of the River Ouse via a gate through the car park. This path will take you back into the city.

Literary York

The eighteenth century saw York's zenith as a social centre for the élite and also its high point as a centre for literature and learning. While the gentry was entertained at York's Theatre Royal, printers published all manner of texts, many from premises in Stonegate. This walk explores the physical locations associated with literature in York, as well as the many references to York in literature of all periods.

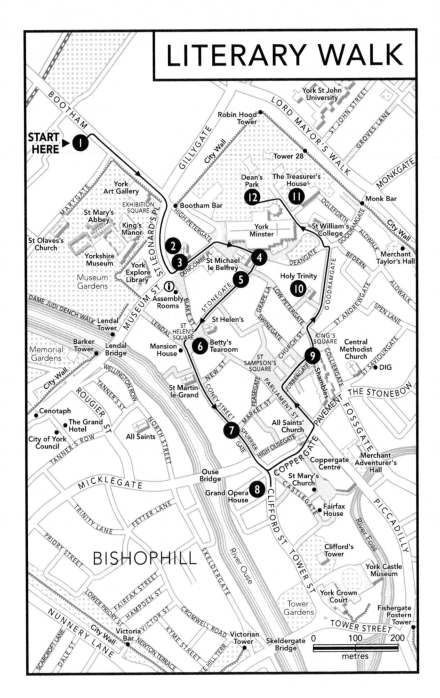

LITERARY WALK

Start: Bootham
End: Dean's Park

1. 54 Bootham

Begin your walk at 54 Bootham, once the home of WH Auden.

Auden was born to George Augustus Auden and Constance Rosalie Auden in this house in 1907. One year later his father accepted a medical position in London. Therefore, his time in York was brief. His poignant and powerful poem Funeral Blues featured in the film Four Weddings and a Funeral.

2. 54 Bootham to York Theatre Royal, St Leonard's Place

Walk towards Bootham Bar. At Exhibition Square in front of the Art Gallery, turn right and follow the road around until you arrive at York Theatre Royal.

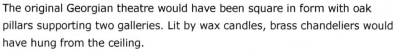

Although the façade of the theatre is Victorian Gothic (1880), the interior incorporates the original theatre of 1734, which was called New Theatre. Granted a royal patent in 1765, it was then given its present name. When York became the social centre for the aristocracy in the eighteenth century, the theatre would have been an important form of entertainment and a place where the gentry could see and be seen.

The original Georgian theatre would have been square in form with oak pillars supporting two galleries. Lit by wax candles, brass chandeliers would have hung from the ceiling.

3. York Theatre Royal to Tate Wilkinson's House

Leave St Leonard's place by walking towards the Tourist Information Centre on Museum Street. At the corner, next to Red House, turn left. Walk beyond Red House to find the small Georgian house tucked between the Red House and the church.

This was once the house of the actor-theatre manager of York Theatre Royal, Tate Wilkinson. Wilkinson arrived in York in 1763 at the age of 26, having gained experienced in London working for the famous theatre manager, Garrick. Renowned for being good fun, Wilkinson was a great mimic of those around him. In 1775 he was put in charge of the Northern Circuit of actors and in 1776 he was able to buy complete control of the theatre, becoming Master of the Theatre Royal. With apparent boundless energy, he also managed satellite theatres in Hull, Wakefield, Leeds, Pontefract, Doncaster and Beverley, all comprising the Yorkshire Circuit. Theatre Royal was the best of the provincial playhouses and Wilkinson was influential in persuading prestigious players to act here. Later he wrote a memoir called "The Wandering Patentee, History of the Yorkshire Theatres", detailing the 36 years during which he ran the theatre. The four-volume book ranks high in theatrical literature of the time. He was clearly a very busy man and

fortunately didn't have far to go to work. Notice the passage between Red House and Tate Wilkinson's house. This would have been the original entrance to York Theatre Royal. It was a squeeze for the gentry to get through in their sedan chairs, so the entrance was moved to St Leonard's Place. The house now forms part of the theatre complex.

3. Tate Wilkinson's House to Red House

Now walk to the left and stand in front of Red House.

Notice the plaque on the bottom left part of the building. This commemorates the fact that the first resident, Dr Burton, was portrayed as Dr Slop by Laurence Sterne in his novel "The Life and Opinions of Tristram Shandy, Gentleman" (1759). One of the earliest novels ever written, "Tristram Shandy" was a huge

success in its day, running to many volumes and re-prints. In it Laurence Sterne lampooned Dr Burton and some believe that this was probably because Burton was a Catholic and Jacobite sympathiser, while Sterne was a cleric in the Anglican church. Although Sterne had livings in Stillington and Coxwold, he spent a lot of time in York, enjoying the various entertainments and pleasures that it afforded.

4. Red House to Minster Gates

Leave Red House by walking towards York Minster. At the main entrance walk to the right and enter Minster Yard. On the right you will notice an exit to the precinct called Minster Gates. Enter Minster Gates and notice the statue of Minerva on the side of the shop on the right of the street.

Minerva is the Roman goddess of wisdom and she sits leaning on a pile of books to advertise the shop. In Georgian times this is where authors and literary readers met as members of one of Britain's earliest book clubs.

5. Minster Gates to Stonegate

Cross Petergate and walk into Stonegate.

As one of the main thoroughfares through York, Stonegate is where you would have found silversmiths, goldsmiths, glass painters and printers in Georgian times.

Find number 35 on the left, above which you will see the sign of the Bible.

The sign of the Bible dates back to 1682 when Francis Hildyard opened a printers and bookshop here. Hildyard printed Laurence Sterne's "Tristram Shandy" and Sterne sometimes lodged in this house on his excursions from the countryside to York. He became a member of the York Club which met in Coney Street Coffee House.

Find number 33 and the sign of the red devil leading into Coffee Yard.

The red devil is the traditional symbol of printers. Devils were the small boys who fetched and carried the type. The printer and publisher Thomas Gent had his workshop at 33 Coffee Yard, helping Stonegate to become known as "The Street of the Printers". In the 17th century cities had to gain a license to print books and in 1662, York was one of the few cities outside London to receive a license. Over the course of the eighteenth century there were at least 13 book-printers active in York, publishing newspapers, pamphlets, books of sermons, advice on household management, accounting, business skills, works of literature, scientific studies, medical treatise and antiquarian research. While Laurence Sterne was propelled to fame, York became perceived as a city of learning and culture.

6. Stonegate to Betty's Tearoom

At the end of Stonegate you will emerge into St Helen's Square. Notice Betty's Tearoom to your left.

Novelist Kate Atkinson was born in York in 1951 and set her debut novel "Behind the Scenes of the Museum" in her hometown. In her novel "Started Early, Took My Dog", the fictional detective Jackson Brodie enjoys a perfectly made cup of coffee in Betty's Tearoom.

7. Betty's Tearoom to Coney Street

Leave St Helen's Square by turning left in front of the pink and white Mansion House and enter Coney Street.

From Victorian times onwards Coney Street housed the print works and headquarters of newspapers based in York, such as the York Herald and the York Courant.

Continue on Coney Street and look for the plaque on the right-hand side that commemorates a visit by Charlotte and Anne Brontë.

Charlotte and Anne Brontë, along with their friend Ellen Nussey, spent the night at the George Inn which stood on this site from 1614. They were on their way to Scarborough where they hoped that the sea air might revive Anne who was suffering from the final stages of tuberculosis. While in York Charlotte bought some bonnets and gloves. The next morning they paid a visit to the Minster, where Anne was overawed by its beauty and in the afternoon they took the train to Scarborough. Unfortunately, Anne died there a few days later on 28th May 1849. Facing her death with great bravery she wrote, "I do long to do some good in the world before I leave it. I have many schemes in my head for future practise - humble and limited indeed- but still I should not like them all to come to nothing, and myself to have lived to so little purpose. But God's will be done". Fortunately, she left us two great works of literature to enjoy - "The Tenant of Wildfell Hall" and the semi-autobiographical "Agnes Grey".

8. Coney Street to the Grand Opera House

Walk to the end of Coney Street until it becomes Spurriergate. Cross the road at the traffic lights, then turn left to walk to the Grand Opera House.

The Grand Opera House was originally built as a Corn Exchange and warehouse in 1868 and was subsequently converted into a theatre for the owner William Peacock in 1902. It opened on January the 20th 1902 with a production of "Little Red Riding Hood". Having cost Peacock £20,000, he ran it with the help of his family until 1945, during which time he put on a great variety of productions including music hall, pantomime, variety, opera, plays, and even some of the early silent films.

9. The Grand Opera House to the Shambles

Walk back towards the centre of the city, cross road and turn right along Coppergate. At Parliament Street take the small street called Jubbergate that leads to the Shambles Market. Look down the Shambles.

This is the street that inspired JK Rowling to create Diagon Alley in "Harry Potter and the Philosopher's Stone". In the novel Hagrid accompanies Harry to Diagon Alley so that he can buy his essential supplies for Hogwarts School. The Shambles is probably the oldest street in Britain and so you will easily be able to imagine

(c) John Robinson

the Leaky Cauldron Pub, Gringotts Bank and Ollivander's Wand Shop.

10. The Shambles to Holy Trinity, Goodramgate

At the top of the Shambles, keep left into King's Square. Cross the square and turn right onto Goodramgate. On your left you will find a stone archway. Walk through it to find Holy Trinity Church and the plaque commemorating the ceremony that took place here between Anne Lister and Ann Walker.

Anne Lister was educated at Manor House School, once located in the King's Manor. For most of her life Anne kept diaries which detailed her daily routine, as well as her lesbian relationships. The diaries were discovered by one of Anne's descendents two hundred years after her death, hidden behind the wooden panelling of her ancestral home, Shibden Hall in Halifax. The 4,000,000 word dairies were nearly destroyed as they were written in code made up of a combination of algebra and Ancient Greek. Fortunately, they were decoded and transcribed in the 1980s and so we have been able to learn about her remarkable life. In 2019 she became the subject of the BBC TV production "Gentleman Jack". York was an important place for Anne as she would come here to socialise with her many contacts. Clearly, this church was also very important to her, as it is where she sanctified her union with Ann Walker at a time when homosexuality was not permitted.

11. Holy Trinity, Goodramgate to the Treasurer's House

Leave Holy Trinity by the same gate that you entered and turn left along Goodramgate. When you reach York Minster, take the cobbled road to the right to arrive at the Treasurer's House. Here you will find a blue plaque to Elizabeth Montagu. Walk along Chapter House Street where you will find Grays Court.

Elizabeth Montagu was born at Grays Court on 2nd October 1718. After the death of her only child in 1744, she founded the celebrated Bluestocking Club "where literary topics were to be discussed, but politics, gossip and card-playing were barred." In 1760 she contributed to "Dialogues of the Dead" - a series of conversations between the living and the famous dead, intended as a satire on 18th century vanity and manners. Dividing her time between her country houses and London, she returned to her hometown in 1742 and was impressed by the Minster, as well as excited to visit the relatively new Assembly Rooms.

12. Grays Court to Dean's Park

Enter Dean's Park opposite the Treasurer's House. Look at York Minster where you will see a stunning grisaille glass window with five panels.

This is the Five Sisters Window that inspired a story in Charles Dickens' novel "Nicholas Nickleby". In the story, Dickens imagines that each of the windows has come to life as a real sister and writes, "five maiden sisters… all of surpassing beauty dwelt in the ancient city of York. Four of them were aged between 22 and 19 but …if the four elder sisters were lovely, how beautiful was the youngest, a fair creature of sixteen!" Dickens used to give readings from his novels. In 1858, he was at the now vanished Festival Concert Rooms, on the corner of Blake Street and Museum Street, where the Tourist Information Office stands today. Well done. You have completed your walk.

Further Information:

York is mentioned in several other works of fiction. The earliest is **Daniel Defoe's** "Robinson Crusoe", first published in 1719. The introduction explains that the main character was born in York. "I was born in the year 1632, in the city of York, to a good family…" In Defoe's "A Tour Through the Whole Island of Great Britain", he wrote, " York is full of gentry and persons of distinction, so they live at large and have houses proportioned to their quality, - nowhere in England was better furnished with provisions of every kind, nor any so cheap in proportion to the goodness of things."

Wilkie Collins, author of "The Woman in White" and "The Moonstone", visited York on a number of occasions and set part of his 1862 novel "No Name" in the city, in which Captain Wragge describes his stroll along the city walls.

Pubs Walk

It has been said that during the medieval period in York, there was a monastery for every day of the week (7), a church for every week of the year (52) and a pub for every day of the year (365). Although somewhat of an exaggeration, in actual fact there were approximately 200 inns and alehouses, which some would still consider a substantial amount. Probably the first brewers of ale for mass public consumption were the monasteries because they ran hostelries for travellers and pilgrims. It was also safer to drink ale than water, as the process killed germs. By the medieval period there was a Guild of Taverners and Vintners and in the 14th century, thirty men from this company were eligible to become Freeman of the City, showing their growing importance. Most early ale houses were private houses and were unregulated. However, by the 15th century some regulation was introduced for tax purposes. By 1832 and the cholera epidemic, York-born Doctor John Snow noticed that those who drank beer were afforded some protection from the illness and he made the link between the disease and contaminated water. So if you stop for a pint in one of the pubs en route, you can always argue that it was for medicinal purposes! As there are so many pubs of historic interest, it has not been possible to include them all. Consequently this walk snakes around the historic centre. Nevertheless, hopefully you will be able to walk in a straight line by the end of it and your walk doesn't literally turn into a pub crawl!

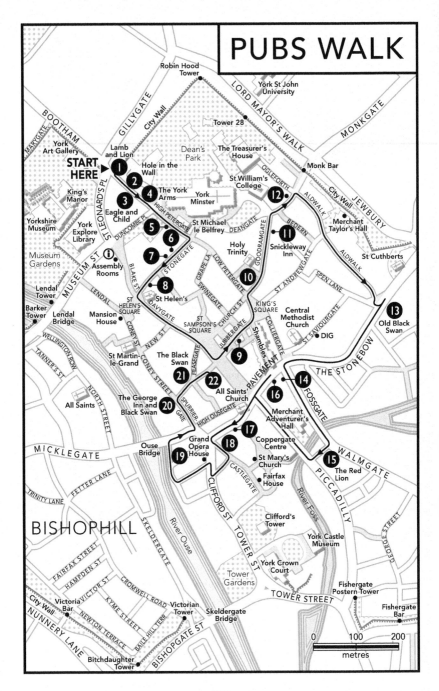

PUBS WALK

Start:	Lamb and Lion, High Petergate
End:	The Burns Hotel, 23 Market Street.

1. Lamb and Lion, High Petergate
Begin your walk at the Lamb and Lion, just within Bootham Bar.

Nestling into the city walls, the original building on this site burnt down in the 17th century. The current building is a townhouse that dates from 1840. There is a pleasant courtyard beer garden to the rear, overlooked by the city walls.

2. The Hole in the Wall, High Petergate
Continue down the street into the city and you will arrive at the Hole in the Wall on the left.

Formerly the Board Inn, there are two theories as to the origin of the present name. Firstly, it could be due to its proximity to the "hole" of Bootham Bar. Or it could be that during excavations in 1816 a hole was discovered in the cellar which led to a dungeon where ghastly chains and manacles were found. The pub is said to be haunted, but don't worry because superstitious builders bricked up the eerie corridor where footsteps were heard.

3. The Eagle and Child, High Petergate
On the right you will see The Eagle and Child.

Built in 1640, this Grade II listed timber- framed pub is spread over three floors. Legend has it that The Rolling Stones once hung out in the top floor bar in the 60s and their signatures in lipstick are still on the wall!

4. The York Arms, High Petergate
Continue towards the city centre on High Petergate.

The present building dates back to 1838 when it incorporated an earlier 18th century house. Prior to becoming a pub it was the Chapter House Coffee House.

5. Guy Fawkes Inn, 25 High Petergate

At the junction continue on High Petergate to the right of St Michael Le Belfry church.

The Guy Fawkes Inn claims to be the birthplace of the notorious Gunpowder plotter because a house to the rear was formerly thought to be his birthplace. Guy Fawkes Cottage at number 26 is attached to the pub and dates from the late 18th century when it was once a workshop and a dwelling. Fawkes was baptised in 1590 at the church of St Michael Le Belfry across the road, although it is more likely that he was born on Stonegate.

6. The House of Trembling Madness, 48 Stonegate

Continue along High Petergate and turn right when you arrive at Stonegate. Find The House of Trembling Madness on the right.

This Grade II listed building dates from 1600 with 19th century alterations and shop front. Covering three storeys, the ground and second floors have their timber frames exposed.

7. Ye Olde Starre Inne, Stonegate

Continue along Stonegate where you will find Ye Olde Starre Inne down an alleyway to the right.

The star may be a reference to the Star of Bethlehem that guided travellers to the Minster or to the crest of the Innkeepers' Company which is a 16-pointed star. It is the oldest continuously licensed premises in York. The main block at the back of the yard is mid 16th century. The first recorded landlord in 1644 was a staunch Royalist and so he would have been none too pleased after the city fell during the siege of York as he would have had to serve Parliamentarians. Originally there was a coaching yard in front which was in-filled with the advent of the railway in 1840. Consequently, the pub is now set back from the main street when the shop front was added. Stables at the rear would have stretched all the way to Duncombe Place. Travelling players would store their wares in these stables, so the pub became the haunt of actors and actresses.

8. The Punch Bowl, 7 Stonegate

Return to Stonegate, turn right and walk until you see the Punch Bowl on your left.

There was a coffee house on this site in 1675 until 1761 when it was granted its license to sell alcohol, making it the fifth oldest pub in York. It evolved into a meeting place for the Whigs, a political party which was the forerunner of the Liberal Party. Whigs enjoyed partaking in a cup of punch, hence the name. (The Tories preferred port and red wines). York Race Committee made it its headquarters and bell-ringers from York Minster were customers in the 18th century. In 1931 it was completely rebuilt.

9. Gert and Henry's, 4 Jubbergate

At St Helen's Church, Stonegate turn right and walk along Davygate. Continue past St Sampson's Square onto Parliament Street. Walk beyond Church Street and Goodramgate. Turn left onto Jubbergate. Here you will find Number 4 Jubbergate.

By 1280 this street was called "Joubrettegat", meaning "the street of the British in the Jewish quarter". This solitary medieval building would once have adjoined others, which have since been demolished. It's two-storey, gabled, timber-frame has been much restored, with a modern extension to the rear.

10. Old White Swan, 80 Goodramgate

Walk along Jubbergate until you leave the Shambles and the market area to arrive at King's Square. Cross the square and head along Goodramgate, out of the city towards Monk Bar. On your left you will find the Old White Swan.

Part timber-framed, the centre of the building ranges from the 16th century. The area set back from the street with side wings is mid 18th century. The frontage was rebuilt in 1771. It is the third oldest continuously licensed pub, first recorded in 1703. Over the years it has been a pigsty, a barber and a barn. In the early 17th century many disputes arose due to the fact that it found itself in two parishes. The solution was to paint a white line through the courtyard and kitchen to show the boundary. In the subsequent centuries it was a major coaching and posting inn. In the days before the railway, farmers and poultry dealers used to congregate here at fixed times to sell their products to city clients.

11. Snickleway Inn, 47 Goodramgate

Continue along Goodramgate where you will find the Snickleway Inn on your right.

At one time the pub was known as the House of Tudor. During the Siege of York in 1644, in the midst of the English Civil War, it was used as the Royalist ammunitions store.

12. The Royal Oak, 18 Goodramgate

Continue along Goodramgate.

The building dates back to the 15th century while there has been a pub on the site since the 17th century. Formerly a coaching inn, it was known as the Blue Boar in 1772, later to become The Blue Pig. Its mock Tudor frontage was added in the 1800s.

13. Old Black Swan, Peaseholme Green

Continue on Goodramgate towards Monk Bar and the outskirts of the city. At Aldwark turn right. At St Saviour's Place turn left. Then turn left onto Peaseholme Green where you will find the Old Black Swan.

The house was the residence of the Bowes family in the 15th and 16th century. William Bowes who was Sheriff in 1402 and later Lord Mayor in 1417 owned it. He endowed St Cuthbert's church across the road. His great grandson, Sir Martyn Bowes, became Lord Mayor of London and was goldsmith to Elizabeth 1. Later it passed to the Thompson family, who also owned the Olde Starre Inne on Stonegate. Henry Thompson was a wine merchant who became Sheriff in 1601. Edward Thompson, born in 1670, used the building as a townhouse. His daughter Henrietta Thompson marred Colonel Edward Wolfe in 1724 and they resided here. In 1726 they moved to Kent where their son, James Wolfe was born. Known as General Wolfe, he died taking Quebec from the French and so laid the foundations of British Canada. The building was not licensed as a pub until the 19th century. The interior is mainly mid-17th century. A very fine staircase leads upstairs to the "Trompe D'Oeil" room where the woodwork is painted to look like elaborate panelling.

14. The Blue Bell, 53 Fossgate

Walk along Peaseholme Green towards the city centre, walk along Pavement until you arrive at Fossgate on the left. Turn down Fossgate and find the Blue Bell on the right.

The Blue Bell is a Grade II listed Edwardian pub with an unaltered interior, the only one to survive in York. Of interest inside are the part-glazed, panelled doors with embossed glass that incorporate the names of each of the rooms. The bar has its original panelled counter and the Smoke Room has a fireplace with Art Nouveau decoration.

15. The Red Lion, Merchantgate

Return to Fossgate, turn right and walk along the street until you arrive at the Red Lion on the corner of Fossgate and Merchantgate.

This pub is built on 13th century foundations with a 14th-15th century superstructure. The two side wings date to 1600. There is reputedly a 13th century bread oven in the front bar. It is the oldest building in York used as pub but has only been licensed since the 19th century. On the first floor there is a priest's hole between two bedrooms. Fossgate leads into Walmgate and at one point in time there would have been a total of 28 pubs on these two streets! Former customers would have frequented the pig market on Foss Bridge.

16. The Golden Fleece, Pavement

Walk along Piccadilly, the street parallel to Fossgate, back in the direction of the city centre. Turn right on Pavement where you will find The Golden Fleece.

Before 1570 this property belonged to the Merchant Adventurers Guild. In 1667 a York merchant, Richard Booth, was allowed to mint his own copper halfpennies here. John Peckett, Lord Mayor in 1702, owned part of the house that adjoins the pub, where he lived with his wife, Lady Alice Peckett, until the late 17th century. The pub was first licensed in 1668 and takes its name from the wool trade, the staple trade of York between the 13th and 17th centuries. The frontage is mid-19th century, but the rear goes back to the 16th century where you will see the remains of a courtyard for coaches.

17. The Three Tuns, 12 Coppergate

Return to Pavement and turn left. Cross Piccadilly and continue until you arrive at The Three Tuns.

The pub was probably built in the 16th century with 19th century alterations and an extension. It is timber-framed, rendered and white-washed with a jettied first floor. It has been licensed as a pub since 1783.

18. The Blue Boar, Castlegate

Continue along Copperagate, away from the city centre. Take the first left onto Castlegate. Find The Blue Boar.

This pub dates from the early 1700s when it was first known as the Robin Hood, later changing its name to Little John in 1893. This was not its only association with outlaws as the body of the notorious highwayman, Dick Turpin, was laid out here in 1739, after being taken down from the gallows at the Knavesmire. In 2012 it changed its name to the Blue Boar.

19. The King's Arms, King's Snaith

Walk along Castlegate and turn right down Friargate. Cross the road and walk down Cumberland Street next to the Grand Opera House. At King's Staith turn right until you reach the King's Arms.

The building dates from the early 17th century and may have been a custom house or warehouse. The thick walls were always designed to protect it from floods. First recorded as a pub in 1783, by the 19th century it was known as Ouse Bridge Inn. Legend has it that the bodies of criminals were laid out here after being hung from old Ouse Bridge. It reverted to its present name in 1794. The inn sign depicts Richard III who was popular in York because he halved the city's tax burden. Regularly inundated, you can see the flood markers on a board by the bar.

20. The George Inn and Black Swan, Coney Street (Defunct)

Go up the stone steps onto Ouse Bridge and turn right. Cross the road and walk along Spurriergate until it becomes Coney Street. On the left you will see a plaque commemorating the George Inn.

The George Inn

In Elizabethan times Ralph Rokeby Esq (d1575), Secretary of the Council of the North, lived in a townhouse on this site. It was first licensed by Thomas Kaye, Sheriff of York in 1614. It had a fantastically decorated frontage with elaborate plasterwork. A major coaching inn in the 18th and early 19th centuries, many notable people stayed here, including the architect of Castle Howard, Vanbrugh while working on the house. Imagine coaches tearing along Coney Street, turning sharply into a narrow entrance to emerge into a quadrangle behind the building. Charlotte and Anne Brontë, along with their friend Ellen Nussey, stayed here overnight in 1849 after arriving by train from Leeds.

21. The Black Swan

On the opposite side of the street would have stood another coaching inn, the Black Swan. In 1706 the first stagecoach from London to York left the Black Swan in Holborn for its York counterpart at 5am. It took four days to arrive. By 1786 mail coaches arrived here and by 1830 eighteen coaches per day left the Black Swan to places as far afield as Hull, Kendal, Leeds and Carlisle. By 1838 the time from London to York was down to 21 hours and there was enough stabling for 100 horses.

22. The Burns Hotel, Market Street

Walk back to Market Street where you will find the Burns Hotel.

This pub was formerly known as the Hansom Cab after the architect Joseph Hansom from York who gave his name to the horse-drawn carriage that he patented in 1834. The pub was substantially rebuilt in the 1960s with Victorian-style panelling. This is the end of your walk. Well done.

Ghostly and Ghastly Walk

During the course York's history you could be put to death in any
number of places. Justice was not just administered by the Crown,
but the Church also, which had three execution sites of its own.
Meanwhile the Crown used the Knavesmire outside the city and
named it Tyburn in honour of the famous execution site in London.
After complaints from visitors to York travelling along the Tadcaster
Road, the last execution took place at Tyburn took place in 1801
when executions moved to York Castle. Until 1868 executions were
a public spectacle, after which they were moved into an area of
the Female Prison. The last execution in York took place in 1896.
As you complete this walk, please spare a thought for the victims
of execution, many of whom were innocent. Some of the stories
are unfortunately very true, others you will have to decide on for
yourself. In 2002, when Ghost Research Foundation International
recorded 594 ghostly presences around the city, they labelled York
as the most haunted city in the world. Here are a few of the spooky
tales that have done the rounds over the years.

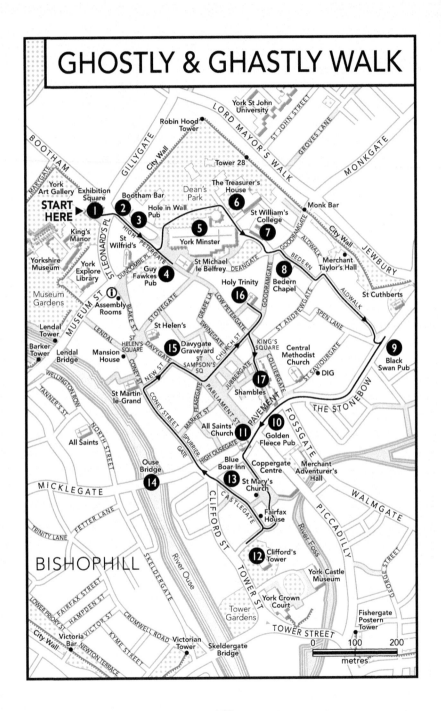

GHOSTLY & GHASTLY WALK

York St John University

BOOTHAM

GILLYGATE

LORD MAYOR'S WALK

ST JOHN STREET

Groves Lane

MONKGATE

Robin Hood Tower

City Wall

Tower 28

York Art Gallery

MARYGATE

Exhibition Square

START HERE ▶ **①**

Bootham Bar **②**

Hole in Wall Pub **③**

Dean's Park

The Treasurer's House **⑥**

St William's College **⑦**

Monk Bar

City Wall

JEWBURY

King's Manor

ST LEONARD'S PL

St Wilfrid's

HIGH PETERGATE

DUNCOMBE PL

York Minster **⑤**

St Michael le Belfrey

DEANGATE

GOODRAMGATE

ALDWALK

BEDERN

Merchant Taylor's Hall

Yorkshire Museum

York Explore Library

Guy Fawkes Pub **④**

St Cuthberts

Bedern Chapel **⑧**

ALDWALK

SPEN LANE

Museum Gardens

MUSEUM ST

Assembly Rooms **ⓘ**

STONEGATE

GRAPE LA

LOW PETERGATE

Holy Trinity **⑯**

GOODRAMGATE

ST ANDREWGATE

Black Swan Pub **⑨**

Lendal Tower

Barker Tower

Lendal Bridge

BLAKE ST

Mansion House

St Helen's

ST HELEN'S SQUARE

LENDAL

DAVYGATE

CONEY ST

NEW ST

Davgate Graveyard **⑮**

ST SAMPSON'S SQ

SWINEGATE

CHURCH ST

KING'S SQUARE

Central Methodist Church

COLLIERGATE

ST SAVIOURGATE

DIG

THE STONEBOW

FOSSGATE

WELLINGTON ROW

TANNER'S ROW

NORTH STREET

St Martin-le-Grand

CONEY ST

Shambles **⑰**

JUBBERGATE

MARKET ST

FEASEGATE

PARLIAMENT ST

PAVEMENT

All Saints' Church **⑪**

Golden Fleece Pub **⑩**

Merchant Adventurer's Hall

WALMGATE

PICCADILLY

All Saints

Ouse Bridge **⑭**

MICKLEGATE

SPURRIER GATE

HIGH OUSEGATE

Blue Boar Inn **⑬**

Coppergate Centre

St Mary's Church

Fairfax House

River Foss

GEORGE STREET

FETTER LANE

TRINITY LANE

CLIFFORD ST

CASTLEGATE

Clifford's Tower **⑫**

BISHOPHILL

LOWER PRIORY ST

FAIRFAX STREET

HAMPDEN ST

VICTOR ST

CROMWELL ROAD

SKELDERGATE

River Ouse

TOWER ST

York Castle Museum

York Crown Court

Tower Gardens

TOWER STREET

Fishergate Postern Tower

City Wall

Victoria Bar

KYME STREET

NEWTON TERRACE

Victorian Tower

Skeldergate Bridge

0   100   200

metres

Start: Exhibition Square

End: The Shambles, the shrine of Margaret Clitherow

1. Exhibition Square

Begin your walk in Exhibition Square in front of the Art Gallery.

In 1642 Catholicism was not tolerated. Eighty-one-year-old Friar John Lockwood was brought from Thornton-Le-Street, strapped across a horse, fainting and vomiting. A scaffold was erected in Exhibition Square and under pressure from his councillors, King Charles 1 signed his death warrant in sight of the scaffold at King's Manor. Lockwood struggled up the ladder and his last words were reportedly, " Who would not labour a little to reach heaven?" Even the crowd was shocked when they were showered with parts of his entrails. Some say that Judge Dodsworth, who was in the crowd, died of a heart attack at the sight of the gruesome execution, while his wife went mad and died later.

2. Bootham Bar

Now look across the road to Bootham Bar.

If you had been standing here in 1663, you would have seen the heads on spikes of three rebels who did not want Charles II to become King of England. The bars of York were often used as depositories for the severed heads of those considered to be traitors. At Micklegate Bar in 1746 you would have seen the heads of two men involved in the Jacobite Rebellion, the attempt to usurp George II and put Bonne Prince Charlie on the throne. The heads remained there as a decaying and putrefying warning to others for seven long years, until one night they disappeared. Rescued by William Arundell, a tailor from York, he paid for his act by being sentenced to two years in prison for theft.

3. Hole in the Wall pub

Go through Bootham Bar and enter the city. On your left you will find the Hole in the Wall pub.

In 1816 excavations at this pub revealed a ghastly secret passage in the cellar, complete with chains and manacles. Eerie footsteps could be heard from time to time. Frightened builders blocked up the entrance to prevent any further ghostly goings-on.

At the end of the road take the fork to the right of the church and continue on High Petergate.

Guy Fawkes was christened at St Michel Le Belfry church, across from the pub, in 1570. After selling his lands in Clifton, he went off to fight for the Catholic King of Spain and in the process became an expert in gunpowder. Captured for his part in the 1605 Gunpowder Plot to blow up James 1 and the House of Parliament, he refused to give up the names of his co-plotters, even under torture. Dragged to his place of execution with three others, Fawkes was the last to stand on the scaffold. He made the sign of the cross and asked for the forgiveness of the King. Weakened by torture and aided by the hangman, Fawkes began to climb the ladder to the noose, but either through jumping to his death or climbing too high so the rope was incorrectly set, he managed to avoid the agony of being hung, drawn and quartered while still alive. After death his body parts were distributed to "the four corners of the kingdom", to be displayed as a warning to other would-be traitors.

5. York Minster

Now stand before York Minster and spare a thought for poor old Archbishop Scrope.

Archbishop Scrope of York set up a rebellion against King Henry IV, making a list of all the things that he wanted the King to change. He preached against the King in the Minster and the people responded by forming an army of around 8,000 men. Henry IV offered Scrope a truce in exchange for disbanding his men. However, this did not protect Scrope from facing the King's wrath. Forced to ride a bony old horse from Bishopthorpe to his place of execution in Skeldergate, he was humiliated even further by being made to face backwards, wearing a blue cloak with a hood. Finally, Scrope was beheaded by a man who had been a prisoner in York for 15 years. He was offered a ghastly bargain. If he axed the Archbishop, then he would be allowed to go free. Rumour has it that four hundred years later, a butcher was driving some sheep along the same road to take them to be slaughtered and sold in his shop. Suddenly the sheep refused to move. The butcher pushed his way through to see why his frightened sheep were stopping. In front of him he saw a coffin being carried along the road. In front of the coffin was a man in a blue robe. Then the butcher blinked. The coffin was following the man... but there was no-one carrying it. It was drifting along. As the butcher tried to get closer to the coffin and the man, they simply faded into the evening air. Archbishop Scrope's tomb can be seen inside the Minster. In 1829 Jonathon Martin hid in York Minster and started a fire, which destroyed the choir and the roof. Found guilty and insane, he died in a madhouse.

6. The Treasurer's House

Enter Dean's Park next to the Minster and walk to the other gate. Leave the park where you will find The Treasurer's House.

In the 1960s it was decided to install a modern central heating system in the house and work was begun in the cellar. Eighteen-year-old apprentice plumber Harry Martindale was doing groundwork in the cellar when suddenly he heard the distant sound of a bugle blowing. He wasn't sure, but it sounded like a trumpet making repeated discordant sounds. Returning to his work, Harry realised that the noise was becoming louder and louder. Then suddenly the torso of a soldier emerged from the wall directly in front of him. Recovering his senses, Harry backed away and huddled in a corner of the room to witness the scene. As he stared in disbelief, soldiers one by one, began to emerge from the wall, striding across the cellar in single file, finally disappearing through the wall at the opposite end of the cellar. The first thing that Harry noticed about the men was that they seemed to be rather short, probably only chest height. On closer inspection, it appeared that the soldiers were actually walking on their knees! He could see nothing at all of their calves, ankles and feet. He noted that they were shabbily dressed and wearing red tunics. Their helmets were plumed like those of the Roman soldiers that he had learnt about in school. They carried round shields on their left arms and some kind of dagger in a scabbard on their right side. The troop appeared tired, as though they had been on the march for days with little rest. Another aspect that particularly struck Harry's mind was that one of the soldiers emerged laid out flat on the back of a carthorse. He couldn't tell if the man was asleep or dead. The ordeal was so terrifying that he had to take several weeks off work. After recounting his experience to family and close friends, the press got hold of the story and reluctantly, Harry agreed to speak to the media. It was not long before the national media became interested. Many began to poke fun at

Harry, rubbishing his story. They claimed his account was a figment of his young imagination. They questioned the details of the story. They said that everyone knew that Roman soldiers didn't wear red tunics. It was common knowledge that they wore green tunics. Nevertheless, the young plumber never wavered in his story and told it exactly the same way to anyone who showed an interest. Unfortunately, Harry was so hurt and humiliated by the treatment that he received at the hands of the media that he refused to speak about his experience anymore. Years passed and when a startling discovery was made, people remembered Harry's story. In 1972 building contractors in York discovered a sewage system and then a Roman road running below the Treasurer's House. The two -thousand -year- old road lay approximately 40 centimetres below the level of the cellar of the Treasurer's house. Could this explain why Harry saw a troop of soldiers with no feet? Was this the reason why the soldiers looked like they were walking on their knees? Archaeologists identified the road as the Via Decumana, which ran to the Roman garrison. Then there was another exciting discovery. A Roman cemetery was excavated, and a piece of cloth was found, which was red, proving that the Romans did wear red. Later in life, asked whether he believed in ghosts Harry said that he "only believed in what he saw." After serving the community as a policeman for the next thirty years, he passed away in October 2014 at the age of 79 with people still as fascinated by his story as ever.

7. St William's College

Walk towards the Minster and notice the timber-framed building on your left.

St William's College was once the dormitory of the Vicars Choral who were chantry priests paid to sing songs for their wealthy patrons in the Minster. They got into trouble and were moved from their accommodation in Bedern to this site, so that a closer eye could be kept on them. Apparently, one night one of their 26 members attacked someone with the blunt end of an axe. Built in 1461, it was named after William Conqueror's great-great grandson William Fitzherbert. In 1550 two brothers lived here. One night a rich priest walked by and the brothers slit his throat and stole his purse. The younger brother was terrified by the crime. The older brother was worried he'd go to the law, so he went himself and told them the younger brother had done it. The younger brother was hanged and never knew who had given him away. It is said that the guilty older brother walks St William's College pathways, moaning due to the guilt he feels at betraying his brother.

8. Bedern Chapel

Cross Goodramgate and find the archway into the alleyway called Bedern on the left-hand side of the street in the direction of the centre of the city.

In the mid 19th century George Pimm was ordered by the church to round up all the orphans and waifs and strays in the area and enroll them in Bedern Ragged School. For each child he housed at the school, Pimm was paid a fee. Not content with this income, he made extra money by renting the children out to work on farms, market stalls and as chimney sweeps. Squalid living conditions ensured that many of the children died of starvation or disease. For every child who died, George Pimm would lose the income from their allowance. To protect his revenue stream, Pimm began to hide the dead children within the grounds and walls of the school, so that the church continued to think that they still lived. Over the eight years that the school was open, Pimm hid at least 13 children in and around the school. Eventually Pimm began to suffer from paranoia and reported a strange atmosphere around the school. He claimed he could hear noises - wailing, tapping and scratching, and turned to alcohol for comfort. Soon he started to tell others of the noises that he had heard, but no-one believed him, blaming the drink. Soon his ramblings reached the church and they decided to investigate. Horrified by the state of the school, they closed it down. Pimm was taken to the lunatic asylum, where he stayed for the rest of his life. After four months of incarceration, he hung himself. In a suicide note he complained of the wailings and screams of the dead children that tortured him in his cell. Visitors to the Bedern area have spoken of feeling their clothing or bags being tugged as they walk through the Bedern Arch. Some people have heard childrens' laughter, whilst others have heard screams of terror.

9. Black Swan, Peaseholme Green

Proceed through Bedern until you arrive at St Andrewgate. Turn left, then turn right and walk down Aldwark. Emerge onto Peaseholme Green where you will see the Black Swan pub.

A house on this site dates back to the fourteenth century, so as you can imagine there are many ghostly goings on in the pub. A ghostly gentleman in a bowler hat appears at the bar occasionally and seems to be waiting for someone, until he fades away. Also, in the bar the ghost of a beautiful young woman has been seen staring into the fire. She is thought to be a jilted bride. A curse hangs upon her whereby if a man stares into her face, he will die in ecstasy. A small boy dressed in Victorian style clothes is frequently seen between the bar and the passageway. Although the staff have affectionately named him Matthew, they suspect he is a pickpocket as objects keep disappearing from behind the bar. Late at night sometimes someone can be heard singing Irish folk songs. Staff suspect that this is Jack, rumoured to be a highwayman, as he is regularly seen in the kitchen in riding boots and a long black cloak. Interestingly, the kitchen was built over the original stable yard. Dare you enter for a drink?

10. Golden Fleece, Pavement

From Peaseholme Green, walk towards to city centre along Pavement. On the left you will find the Golden Fleece.

With the building dating back to 1503, the Golden Fleece claims to be the most haunted pub in York. Lady Alice Peckett, the wife of the Mayor of York, has been seen walking the corridor that adjoins her house to the pub. One-eyed Jack wears leather boots and a red jacket from the 16th century. He always packs a pistol and has been spotted at the bottom bar. A soldier from World War II is also said to haunt one of the rooms upstairs. While lodging in the room, he fell from the window to the street below. Those who have stayed in the room subsequently have sensed his presence.

11. All Saints Church, Pavement

From the Golden Fleece walk to the left to the church with the lantern tower. Inside the church can you find the sword, helmet and gauntlets pinned to the wall?

This is a replica of the sword of Thomas Percy, 7th earl of Northumberland who was beheaded on Pavement in 1572 in what was then the marketplace, on the orders of Elizabeth I for seeking to have Mary, Queen of Scots become queen during the Pilgrimage of Grace. Although he fled to Scotland, he was captured and sold to the English government. Dragged to York in chains, he refused to abandon his religion. His sword was ceremoniously broken to symbolise his treachery. His body was buried in an unmarked grave by his servants and he is still said to roam the graveyards of York looking for his head.

12. Clifford's Tower

From the church, cross Coppergate and enter the Coppergate Centre. Walk through the Coppergate centre and leave by the exit next to the department store and the ice cream shop. Continue forward until you arrive at Clifford's Tower.

Clifford's Tower is on the site of York Castle, which has been the site of the administration of justice since the Norman times in the 11th century. The patch of grass between the Castle Museum, the Court and the Female Prison is called "The Eye of York" and public executions have been held here over the centuries. St George's Field where the car park is by the river was also used as a place of execution. Clifford's Tower has also been the scene of gruesome bodies dangling in cages as deterrents to potential offenders.

Robert Aske objected to Henry VIII's Dissolution of the Monasteries (1536) and headed a Pilgrimage of Grace consisting of nine thousand rebels. Although he received the promise of safe passage to London to meet Henry VIII to discuss matters, it was not to be. After being convicted of high treason in Westminster, he was taken back to York, hung in chains on a special scaffold erected outside Clifford's Tower and left to die of hunger, thirst and exposure.

13. Blue Boar Inn

Walk back towards the city centre along Castlegate.

As you walk along Castlegate, imagine slums on your left going down to the River Ouse. Also imagine prisoners being publically paraded from the castle complex in carts to the place of their execution. Stop when you arrive at the Blue Boar on your right.

In 1739 Dick Turpin, the notorious highwayman, was publically paraded along Castlegate all the way to the Knavesmire, the place of his execution. In a show of bravado, he bowed to the crowds which lined the route. A proud man, he had bought himself a new set of clothes for the occasion and hired six paid mourners. After his death his body was taken down and brought here to the Boar Inn where it was laid out for the ordinary people to view it. Ruthless body snatchers lay in wait wanting to perform medical experiments upon the fresh corpse. While the customers of the pub saved the body from the doctor, they could not protect it from being dug up by a labourer who sold it to a surgeon. When the mob found out what had happened, they descended on the surgeon's house and the doctor and labourer were arrested. Marmaduke Palms was bound over for trying to take the body for anatomical dissection. Turpin's body was then reburied, and his coffin filled with unslaked quicklime to prevent any further exhumations. Hopefully, he now rests in peace! (You can see his headstone in St George's churchyard.)

14. Ouse Bridge

Walk towards the junction of Nessgate, Coney Street and Bridge Street.

Look down the street at Ouse Bridge. By 1810 the original medieval bridge over the river had become crowded with houses and shops and so it was replaced. Also lurking under the bridge was a small prison, known as a kidcote lock-up, where all manner of people were held in appalling conditions. In 1694 Frances Bedingfield, the head nun of Bar Convent, was imprisoned for her religious beliefs. This was not the first time that she had to suffer under the bridge. The prison was particularly dangerous as it was prone to flooding with the rise in the water level of the Ouse. If you didn't drown, you might catch a disease from the unsanitary water of the river.

15. Davygate Graveyard

From the junction, walk along Spurriergate, which becomes Coney Street and take the second right onto New Street. You will emerge onto Davygate where you will find some gravestones in the recess on the left.

You might think that it is unusual to find gravestones in the middle of the shopping centre of a city and you would be right. These tombstones would once have been found in the cemetery outside St Helen's church in St Helen's Square ahead. They were moved in the 18th century to allow better access to the Assembly Rooms on Blake Street. Are you able to construct your own ghost story from any of the details on the headstones?

16. Holy Trinity, Goodramgate

Walk back towards St Sampson's Square. Turn left along Church Street, then take Goodramgate, again on the left. Find the archway to Holy Trinity church.

At dusk, just before the gates of the churchyard close, the faint outline of a man has been sighted in this graveyard. He wears fine clothes from the Elizabethan era, leather boots and a wool jerkin. However, above his ruffle, there is no head. Wandering he bends down and appears to try to dig up the earth, appearing to be looking for something. People believe that it can only be the ghost of Thomas Percy, 7th earl of Northumberland, still desperately looking for his severed head, after losing it on Pavement in the sixteenth century.

17. Shambles, Margaret Clitherow

Return to Goodramgate, turn left and walk to King's Square. Cross the square and arrive at the Shambles. Walk down the Shambles until you arrive at the shrine to Margaret Clitherow on the right-hand side of the street.

Born in 1556 Margaret Clitherow converted to Catholicism in 1571 and married John Clitherow, a wealthy butcher where they lived opposite this shrine in numbers 10 and 12. She hid priests in her house and had the Mass said in secret, which was very dangerous when England was in imminent danger of invasion by the Catholic super-power Spain, and Catholic priests were seen as spies. She was imprisoned several times in York Castle. On 12th March 1586 she was arrested for harbouring Jesuits and allowing Mass to be said in her house. She was tried in the Guildhall, but refused to plead, to protect her children and associates from being called as witnesses. For refusing to plead she was condemned to 'peine forte et dure' (long and hard pain), originally a torture designed to make people accept trial by jury. On Ouse Bridge a sharp stone was placed under her back, a door was placed on top of her with progressively heavier stones piled on top of it. Her torture would have lasted for fifteen minutes. Later her body was thrown on the public dunghill where her friends rescued her corpse. Four hundred and fourteen years later, she was canonized by Pope Paul VI in 1970. Your walk ends here, in this peaceful place, giving you the opportunity to reflect on exactly what it means to be a traitor and to die for your beliefs.

Chocolate Walk

York's chocolate story has its origins in the manufacture of confectionary. The businesses of both the Rowntrees and the Terrys had their roots in confectionary. The Rowntrees learnt from the already established Tukes and Joseph Terry Senior adapted his pharmaceutical knowledge to create sugared sweets and lozenges, with Terry's later evolving into chocolatiers under the direction of Joseph Terry Junior. While other northern cities were transformed into industrial powerhouses, York's chocolate economy thrived due to the advent of the railway in 1839 and the use of River Ouse for the importation of raw materials from overseas. This walk traces the history of confectionary and chocolate in the city up to the present day, with ideas for extensions to the outskirts of the city to experience more of the legacy that the "Kings of Chocolate" left behind.

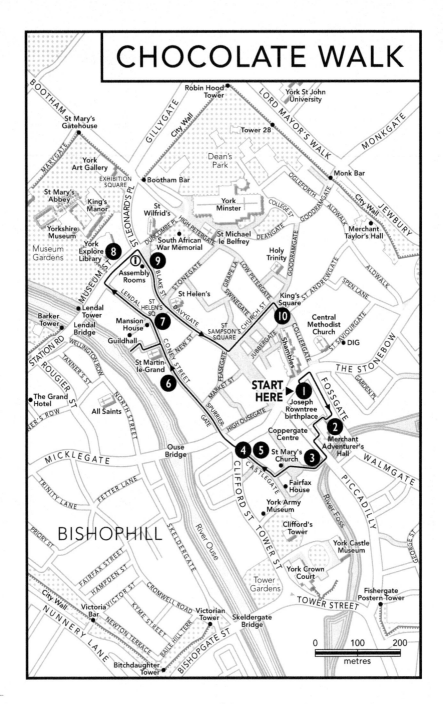

CHOCOLATE WALK

124

Start: 28 Pavement, Joseph Rowntree birthplace.

End: King's Square

1. 28 Pavement

Begin your walk at the plaque commemorating the birthplace of Joseph Rowntree, Junior at 28 Pavement.

Joseph Rowntree, Senior (1801-1859) had his original grocer's shop in a handsome Georgian building on this site. All his other sons were also born here, including Henry Isaac who was Joseph Rowntree Junior's partner before dying prematurely at the age of 45. By 1845 Joseph Senior's business interests were so prosperous that the family was able to move to a handsome townhouse in Bootham, where there is a blue plaque today. After the family left, the shop continued to trade and amongst its apprentices were George Cadbury and Lewis Fry from the Bristol Quaker Chocolate factory.

2. 28 Pavement to Merchant Adventurer's Hall, Fossgate

With your back to the building turn right and right again to walk along Fossgate. Find the small arched entrance to the Merchant Adventurer's Hall on Fossgate on the right.

This is the guild hall of the company of the Merchant Adventurers dating from 1357. This company-controlled trade in the city of York for hundreds of years. In order to be able to trade in the city, you had to be a Freeman of the guild. The only way a woman could join was if she was a widow or a daughter of one of the members. Consequently, when Mary Tuke set up her grocer's shop a little further down the road on Walmgate in 1725, the guild tried to ruin her business by taking her to court, fining her and ordering her to sell up. Mary fought back and after a struggle of approximately eight years, was finally allowed to keep her shop. Joseph Rowntree Senior's son, Henry Isaac was friends with her great-nephew, Samuel, and went to work for Tuke and Co in the 1850s. Having pioneered the sale of drinking chocolate in her shop, Mary is credited with being one of the founders of York's chocolate story.

3. Merchant Adventurer's to Coppergate

Leave the Merchant Adventurer's via the Piccadilly exit. Cross Piccadilly and enter the tunnel that leads to the car park. Walk through the tunnel to emerge into Coppergate.

Mary Ann Craven's (1826-1900) factory, the French Almond Works, was on this site where Yorvik Viking experience stands. By 1881 the factory employed 100 people. In 1966 the premises moved to a larger site to accommodate its expanding workforce and production. Craven's also had four retail shops dotted around York and a popular product was "Mary Ann's Dairy Toffee" as well as "Original French Almonds", which was made to a secret formula brought back from France by one of her sons. If you cross the road and enter All Saints church, Pavement, you will see a beautiful stained-glass window in Mary Craven's honour, commissioned by her family.

4. Coppergate to Castlegate

Leave Coppergate by the side of St Mary's church to emerge onto Castlegate. Turn right and walk to find York Cocoa House on the left.

Originally located in Blake Street as a recreation of a Georgian Coffee House, Sophie Jewett and her partner opened the current site in 2011 in order to be able to share the chocolate manufacturing process with their customers. They provide a range of workshops and training sessions, as well as selling their chocolate products. The founders were inspired to begin their business by their love of chocolate and the unique heritage of York as the home of chocolate production.

Optional Visit: www.yorkcocoahouse.co.uk

5. Castlegate

While on Castlegate consider that at number 20 Castlegate the original factory of Tuke and Co once stood. In 1851 it was listed as "Tuke, Samuel and Co, wholesale tea and coffee dealers". In 1862 it was purchased by Henry Isaac Rowntree and became the site of Rowntree production, until the building was demolished after Henry and Joseph Junior moved to premises on Tanner Moat, a site they chose for its proximity to the old Railway Station. Both buildings have since been demolished.

6. Castlegate to Coney Street

Walk towards the junction of Nessgate, Bridge Street and Spurriergate. Walk along Spurriergate until it becomes Coney Street. Just before St Martin's church, turn left and walk along the paved area until you arrive at the railings overlooking the River Ouse.

As you look ahead you will see North Street at the other side of the river.

North Street is where the brothers Joseph Rowntree Junior and Henry Isaac had a warehouse, near their new factory on Tanner Moat. Henry Isaac was a very hands-on boss and was often seen with his shirtsleeves rolled up on the factory floor. He was relieved when his brother Joseph, more adept at book-keeping and finance, joined him in the business. After Henry Isaac died unexpectedly of an infection in his forties, it was Joseph Rowntree Junior who expanded the chocolate empire, taking it to new heights, as well as continuing the important philanthropic work begun by their father. Their Quaker values encouraged them to adopt ethical business practices that are a blueprint for successful commercial enterprises to this day. The warehouse was razed to the ground in 1942 during the German Baedeker aerial bombardment.

7. Coney Street to St Helen's Square

Return to Coney Street and continue towards the heart of the city where you will find the Mansion House and St Helen's Square.

The Mansion House is the home of the Mayor of York. In 1914 the Lord Mayor sent a bar of chocolate to every British soldier in World War One. An original tin can still be seen inside today.

With your back to the Mansion House look at the building on the left-hand corner of the square. This was the signature shop of the Terry chocolate business.

In the 1820s Joseph Terry Senior opened this shop to take advantage of the 30,000 shoppers who visited York each day. The top floor housed a ballroom and restaurant, while the confectionary shop was on the ground floor. It became one of seventy-five retail outlets owned by the company, which were passed down to Joseph Terry Junior on the death of his father in 1850. Joseph Terry Junior became Lord Mayor of York four times and was knighted in 1887 for his philanthropic work and contribution to the city. In 1898 he died of heart failure at the age of 70, while campaigning to become MP for York. Eventually Terry's was bought by Kraft and production moved to eastern Europe.

Opposite Terry's you will see Betty's Tearoom.

Here they have been handcrafting chocolate from Venezuelan criollo beans for nearly one hundred years. In 1907 a young Swiss baker and confectioner, Fritz Bützer, left his home to travel to England with a dream of establishing his own business. After successfully establishing a Betty's in Harrogate, in 1937 he decided to open a shop in York, directly opposite Terry's to capitalise on York's emergence as the chocolate capital of England.

8. St Helen's Square to York Explore Library.

Leave St Helen's Square via the street that continues from the Mansion House (Lendal) and cross over the road at the end. At the Museum Gardens turn right to find the public library set back from the road.

Joseph Rowntree Senior and Joseph Rowntree Junior were both great philanthropists and advocates of universal education. Joseph Rowntree Senior was a teacher in an Adult School, which emerged to help people overcome illiteracy. He was also one of the people who paid a subscription to create a library. Over time this evolved into the public library that we can all enjoy to this day. There is a plaque to commemorate his contribution in the foyer of the building.

9. York Explore Library to Blake Street

Leave the library and walk up Museum Street towards the Tourist Information Office. At the corner turn right onto Blake Street.

Opposite the Assembly Rooms, on the left you will see a Georgian building. Until 2011 this housed York Cocoa House, a modern tribute to coffee houses that became popular in the 1700s, which sold coffee and hot chocolate. While some women owned and ran Coffee Houses, it was predominantly men who would meet in these cafés to read the newspaper and discuss the issues of the day.

10. Blake Street to King's Square

Walk along Blake Street and return to St Helen's Square. Continue along Davygate and walk beyond St Sampson's Square. Turn left at Church Street. Keep left onto Goodramgate until it opens out into King's Square.

On the right you will find York Chocolate Story. Here you can take a guided tour to learn how York became the chocolate city.

Optional Visit: www.yorkchocolatestory.com

Optional Excursions:

1. Fairfax House, Castlegate.

Visit Fairfax House to see the antique furniture collection of Joseph Terry's great-grandson, Noel Terry, which has been generously lent to York Civic Trust after its restoration of the Georgian house of the 9th Viscount Fairfax.

2. Rowntree Wharf, Hungate

Originating as a flour mill in 1860, Rowntree Wharf consists of five stories with a nine-storey water tower. In 1935 it became the Rowntree and Co's Navigation Warehouse. Gradually as road transport replaced river transport, it fell out of use. Cocoa beans were brought to the wharf until the 1960s. In 1989 it was converted into flats and offices by the Joseph Rowntree Foundation. Accessible via Hungate and along the River Foss.

3. Homestead Park, Clifton

The son of Joseph Rowntree Junior, the social reformer Benjamin Seebhom Rowntree lived in Homestead House from 1904 to 1936. It is now the head office of the Joseph Rowntree Foundation and the park is open to the public. Accessible by walking along the River Ouse from the bank below the Museum Gardens to the north. (1.3 miles)

4. Joseph Rowntree Park, Bishopthorpe

Opened in 1921 by Joseph Rowntree Junior, it was created in memory of Rowntree employees who died in World War I. The gates at the riverbank entrance are eighteenth-century and were given by the company as a memorial to the people of York who died in World War II. Accessible by walking along the River Ouse from King's Staith to Millennium Bridge. (0.8 miles)

5. Terry Factory, Bishopthorpe

In 1926 Joseph Terry Junior moved production to this iconic factory with its 135-foot clock tower. It was inspired by the design of the Woolworth building in New York. The final shift was completed in 2005 when production moved to state-of-the-art premises in Haxby Road. Accessible from the Knavesmire on Tadcaster Road or via Joseph Rowntree Park to Bishopthorpe. (1.4 miles)

6. Goddards, Tadcaster Road

This is the Arts and Crafts home of Noel Goddard Terry who inherited the Terry chocolate empire. Designed by Walter Brierley, it sits in four acres of gardens. Accessible by walking from Micklegate and continuing until Tadcaster Road. (1.4 miles)

www.nationaltrust.org.uk/goddards-house-and-garden

7. New Earswick

Joseph Rowntree Junior built this charming model village between 1902 to 1904. Beginning with 28 houses for both workers and managers, each home had a garden with two fruit trees. Joseph Rowntree's objective was to establish "rightly ordered and self-governing communities". The number 1 bus leaves from Exhibition Square. (2.1 miles)